CREATING crochet fabric

CREATING crochet fabric

experimenting with HOOK, YARN & STITCH

DORA OHRENSTEIN

LARK BOOKS

A Division of Sterling Publishing Co., Inc.
New York / London

senior editor: Terry Taylor

editors: Nathalie Mornu & Larry Shea

technical editor: Karen Manthey

art director: Kathleen Holmes

illustrator: Orrin Lundgren

photographer: Stewart O'Shields

cover designer: Chris Bryant

Library of Congress Cataloging-in-Publication Data

Ohrenstein, Dora, 1949-
   Creating crochet fabric : experimenting with hook, yarn & stitch
/ Dora Ohrenstein.—1st ed.
      p. cm.
   Includes index.
   ISBN 978-1-60059-331-4 (pb-pbk. : alk. paper)
   1. Crocheting. I. Title.
 TT820.O363 2009
 746.43'4—dc22
                                        2008052579
10 9 8 7 6 5 4 3 2 1

First Edition

Published by Lark Books, A Division of Sterling Publishing Co., Inc.
387 Park Avenue South, New York, NY 10016

Text © 2010, Dora Ohrenstein
Photography © 2010, Lark Books, a Division of Sterling Publishing Co., Inc.,
unless otherwise specified
Illustrations © 2010, Lark Books, a Division of Sterling Publishing Co., Inc.,
unless otherwise specified

Distributed in Canada by Sterling Publishing, c/o Canadian Manda Group,
165 Dufferin Street, Toronto, Ontario, Canada M6K 3H6

Distributed in the United Kingdom by GMC Distribution Services,
Castle Place, 166 High Street, Lewes, East Sussex, England BN7 1XU

Distributed in Australia by Capricorn Link (Australia) Pty Ltd.,
P.O. Box 704, Windsor, NSW 2756 Australia

If you have questions or comments about this book, please contact:
Lark Books
67 Broadway
Asheville, NC 28801
828-253-0467

Manufactured in China

ISBN 13: 978-1-60059-331-4

For information about custom editions, special sales, or premium and
corporate purchases, please contact the Sterling Special Sales Department at
800-805-5489 or specialsales@sterlingpub.com.

Contents

Introduction

A FEW YEARS AGO I reconnected with crochet after a twenty-year hiatus. The new yarns I discovered were delightful, and the idea of making lovely garments from my own imagination inspired me to delve deeper. I didn't think of this as "designing," just as a fun hobby.

I began to make swatches—not for gauge, but to discover how the yarns I loved behaved with different stitch patterns and hooks. After several years of serious play with yarns, I've gained new perspectives on the interplay of yarn, hooks, and stitch patterns in crochet fabric. I like to call what I've learned the *fabricology* of crochet. I'm sharing what I learned with you in this book.

We need a book like this one today, because the classic stitch patterns we love were, for the most part, invented on tiny threads, and don't always translate to fuzzy kid mohairs, shiny ribbon yarns, or chunky wool blends. Anyone who's tried a bouclé or tape yarn with a fancy stitch pattern knows just what I mean!

You may already be a very fine stitcher and pattern reader, but do you yearn to create your own designs? Are you reluctant to try yarns that are unfamiliar? Are there stitch patterns and techniques you want to use but you're not sure how? I think this book will get your creative juices flowing and take your skills to the next level.

The book is divided into five distinct, yet interrelated, chapters. After all, nothing in crochet is isolated . . . it's all about the interplay of hook, yarn, and stitch. Throughout the book, you'll find swatches made especially to illustrate the points being discussed. You'll see the same stitch pattern with three or four distinctly different yarns, or the same yarn made up with several stitch patterns. Some of my favorite patterns reappear in numerous swatches, and there's a stitch dictionary for you at the end of the book with patterns you may not have seen before.

In the first chapter, we'll take an in-depth look at the materials and basic tools we work with in crochet—yarns and fibers, and, of course, hooks. I've used some treasures from my stash to create the Ariadne Scarf, made of attached medallions in graduated sizes. You'll be using your own stash, so this project will teach you, in a very hands-on way, how to handle different weights and textures of yarn and how to choose hooks for them.

Next we'll explore two important qualities of crochet fabric: visual structure and drape. The first is about how stitches and texture create visual definition, and the second is about how the fabric moves and feels. I've designed the Rusalka Wrap, using a variegated yarn and a ripple pattern, to drape gracefully around your shoulders, and Papagena's Pouch, a handbag featuring the Basketweave Stitch, to create a much more sturdy and structured fabric.

I'm madly in love with my stitch dictionaries, but I have been foiled many a time when trying to match a pattern with just the right yarn. In the third chapter, we'll analyze the characteristics of stitch patterns from several angles—geometry, density and scale, and intricacy or simplicity—all of which can help determine which yarns they'll work with. Tosca's Lace Tunic mixes an intricate pattern with a simple one in an elegant garment. The Aida Table Mats transform spike stitches into an African textile, and the Lucia Scarf features a brightly colored plaid made with soft mohair yarn.

I hope to change your mind about swatching in the next chapter—that is, swatching for creativity, not to match a pattern's gauge. Nothing is more fun for me in crochet than exploring with swatches. I'll give you tips on what to do with chenille, variegated, self-striping, ribbon, bouclé, and bulky yarns, and how to show them off by choosing a compatible stitch and hook combination. Two different shawls and a hat made with an unexpected stitch pattern will encourage you to seek new uses for special yarns, and handle stitch patterns with flair.

The final chapter is about putting what you've learned into practice. I've created three versatile, wearable designs, each worked in two completely different yarns: two classic Tunisian jackets, two adorable shrugs, and two unique hats. You'll see how the yarn impacts on a design, a valuable lesson to learn. So often when we make a pattern with a substitute yarn, the results are not what we expected. At the same time, you'll discover that adding or subtracting a few rows and stitches is simpler than most people imagine.

I'm assuming that you're a curious, adventurous, and creative person who wants to understand more deeply the craft we both love. As a singer and an opera lover, I know that a role

sung by one singer will be very different from another singer's interpretation. In the same way, I think everyone's crochet can be a highly individual, personal expression. Crochet, like singing, is an interpretive art. In both, there's a tradition we feel connected to, yet we also want to make it our own, to take it to new heights, and to explore the new and untried. The lessons you learn in this book are meant to honor what's come before and help guide your way to as yet unimagined possibilities.

The Materials
& Tools We Use

Yarn, Hook & Stitch

We all know those three words describe the essential tools and techniques for crochet. But those three words don't begin to describe what we have to consider when we assemble our materials. Yarns are categorized by weight, fiber, color, or type of spin and structure. Hooks are labeled with no less than three size designations, and are made from a variety of materials. Crochet stitch patterns number in the thousands and are usually presented in well-established categories, among them lace, closed stitches, raised stitches, clusters, and textured stitches.

Having this enormous array of possibilities to choose from is a huge treat, but it can also be bewildering. How do you choose the right yarn for your project, and which stitch and hook will make it come out the way you imagine it? Yarn, hook, and stitch pattern interact in infinite ways, and getting a handle on that interplay leads to mastery in crochet. Whatever we crochet, we're making a fabric with a specific purpose—whether a cuddly scarf or sweater, a dressy little purse, a sturdy shopping bag, or a cozy blanket. We want that fabric to perform its function well, and in a way that's pleasing to the eye.

Crochet fabric can be as light and gossamer as flower petals, or as sturdy and durable as animal skin. Everything in between is possible, too. It's enough to inspire a whole course of study, and that's why I've coined the term *fabricology*. In this book, we'll examine, dissect, and analyze the variables of crochet, those essential tools that we need to understand and master. Getting a grip on crochet *fabricology* will give us the ability to work with many different types of yarns to produce a fabric that's exactly right for its intended job, and that looks great doing it.

Stitch patterns for swatches marked with

can be found starting on page 120.

fab′·ric·ol′·o·gy the study of the structure and appearance of fabric, esp. with reference to the manipulation of hook, yarn, and stitch pattern in creating crochet fabric.

Today's Yarns

What's different about modern yarns versus those that were available when crochet was invented? First, their size. Early crochet was mostly thread crochet, and intricate stitch patterns were developed on thin, plain yarns made of cotton and linen.

Today, yarns are much heavier. Also striking is the astonishing array of fibers, thicknesses, structures, and colors available in contemporary yarns. As textile technology has grown in sophistication, so have the possibilities for creative and ingenious yarn designs with distinctive characters and complex personalities, from compliant to temperamental, subtle to flamboyant. The new yarns are like people we want to get to know better, and we do that by working them on the crochet hook. It's the tool that unlocks a yarn's character and secrets.

Every season, yarn companies introduce ever more dazzling and seductive new products, some with real benefits in how they handle, others merely catering to the latest fads. It all adds up to irresistible temptation for the yarn lover; going into a yarn shop is like being a kid in a candy store again! If all the new products fill you with as much trepidation as anticipation, then there are many ways to increase your knowledge and gain confidence. Before deciding what to do with any ball of yarn, you should know a few things about it to help you decide what it's best suited for.

Animal Fibers

Fiber content is probably the first thing to consider in a yarn. Many are made from animal fibers: wool from sheep, angora from rabbits, cashmere and mohair from goats, alpaca from its namesake. Nowadays, more exotic animals such as yak, musk ox, and camel are also sources for animal fibers. Animal fibers are often blended with one another in commercial yarns in an effort to overcome any natural shortcomings and enhance the overall practicality and wearability of the yarn.

Wool is the most common hand-knitting yarn fiber, prized for its warmth, elasticity, strength, and durability. There are many varieties of sheep, and thus of wools. Merino and Shetland wools, for example, come from sheep bred specially to produce a softer fiber that strokes the skin. Wool doesn't react well to the agitation of the washing machine, so it's sometimes chemically treated to produce superwash wool that can take rougher treatment.

Mohair, a lustrous and very strong fiber, comes from the Angora goat; its most luxurious form, kid mohair, is shorn from goats no more than 18 months old. It's fuzzy stuff, but there's plenty of variation in fuzz factor depending on the yarn and how it's processed and spun.

Alpaca, which comes from a camelid animal bred in Peru, is a particularly soft, silky yarn. Its most luxurious incarnation, royal alpaca, was originally developed to clothe Incan royalty; it was the cashmere of its time. It's four times warmer than sheep wool, but it has one potential drawback—a tendency to stretch—so many yarn companies blend it with more stable wool to counter this.

Cashmere comes from the Kashmir goat of the Himalayas, which grows an undercoat of hair one-third the diameter of the finest human hair, yielding a highly coveted fiber that's light as a feather yet warmer than wool. Each animal grows no more than 100 grams of this hair annually, which accounts for its high price.

Angora, from the Angora rabbit, is equally soft, but it's not a very strong yarn and it sheds flagrantly. It's generally blended with other fibers in yarn. Of all the animal fibers, its harvesting is the least invasive to the creature because the fibers are simply combed off.

Silk is an animal fiber of a different type. The silk moth caterpillar secretes a long thread to form its cocoon. For the highest grades of silk yarn, manufacturers unwind this long filament in a labor-intensive process called reeling, then twist filaments together. The reeling method yields a waste product out of which lower-grade spun silk is made. The various grades of silk and their processing methods result in a wide array of silk yarns, from soft, lustrous, and smooth to textured, dull, and stiff. Naturally, price tags vary accordingly.

Cellulose Fibers

Cellulose fibers, which derive from vegetable matter, make up the other large category of natural yarn sources. Cotton is the most common, with linen and hemp following behind. The tendency of cellulosic fibers to draw heat away from the body—as opposed to the insulating properties of animal fibers—is what makes them suitable for warm weather. Cellulose fibers are less stretchy on the hook than wool is, yet the fabric is more likely to stretch over time.

Cotton yarns come in a variety of weights, from very thin thread to worsteds. Because stitched-up cotton is heavy, it's best to use a thinner weight for a wearable item. Mercerized cottons have been processed to enhance dye absorption and come in brilliant hues. Egyptian cotton is treasured for its high quality, due to the longer fibers of this specially bred strain. Pima cotton is another special type that's notably softer than other cottons.

Linen fiber, derived from a tall grass called flax, has been used in crochet since Victorian times. It's making a comeback as manufacturers succeed in softening its rigidity and blending it with complementary fibers. Linen is brilliant in color, very strong and durable, and softens considerably with each washing. Its relative stiffness lends great clarity to lacework.

Hemp is even stronger and stiffer, making it a good choice for items such as bags and rugs, where ruggedness is an asset.

Rayon, sometimes called **viscose**, is made from plants and trees and is known as a regenerated fiber. The manufacturing process begins by steaming and chemically treating wood chips, which turns the cellulose into a semiliquid. Forcing this liquid through a spinneret (a device similar to a shower head) creates long filaments, which are then spun into yarn. Newer cellulosic fibers have been generating plenty of interest lately; these include yarns derived from soy pulp, bamboo, and corn. The fact that they're made from renewable sources and tend to be luminous and lightweight makes them attractive. Depending on how they're blended and spun, these yarns all have individual characters.

Synthetics & Organics

Purely synthetic fibers such as acrylic are made from polymers, a long chain of molecules made by chemical synthesis. These can be manipulated to mimic the characteristics of natural fibers, such as appearance and hand, but they don't breathe like the real thing. Acrylic is often blended with natural fibers to enhance the yarn's durability. Synthetic yarns are washable, easy to care for, and generally cheaper than natural fibers.

Top row left to right: Alpaca, Corriedale locks (sheep), cotton roving, and Tencel®
Bottom row left to right: Bamboo, angora (rabbit), tussah silk, and mohair locks (goat)

From Fiber to Yarn

Chemicals are used extensively at every stage of dyeing and processing of yarns: fleece is cleaned with chemical detergents, fibers are bleached and sprayed with synthetic oils, and an array of chemicals is used for dyeing. In today's eco-conscious world, some smaller mills have moved away from chemical processing.

Organic yarns, drawn from animals grazed on natural grasses and cotton grown without pesticides are becoming popular. Organic yarns are undyed and offered in a range of muted colors. So strong is the interest in all things organic today that most large companies now offer organic yarns as well as synthetics.

If you enjoy working from vintage pattern books, you'll find that the weight of yarns is identified by the number of plies. Unfortunately, this isn't a reliable indication of a yarn's weight today. Singles come in a wide variety of thicknesses, and therefore a three- or four-ply yarn can be very thin fingering weight, or much heavier. When working vintage patterns, it's wise to start with a lightweight yarn, and be prepared to adjust stitch and row counts.

Whatever their origin, most fibers are spun before becoming thread or yarn. Spinning is a very ancient art; artifacts date back 20,000 years. Fibers were first twisted by hand, then with the spindle and spinning wheel. Today, hand spinning has an avid and growing following, while commercial yarns are produced at huge industrial mills that serve the textile industry. The same mills often produce yarns for hand knitting, which represents a tiny subsection of the yarn industry.

Before spinning, animal fibers are combed and carded to remove knots and impurities, then drawn out into strips and lightly spun to become roving. Individual strands of fiber are then spun together tightly to create **single-ply yarns**, called singles. In **two-ply yarns**, two singles are twisted together in the opposite direction from how they were originally spun, allowing excess twist to be released and resulting in a stronger, more balanced yarn. **Three-ply yarns** create yet more stability and strength and are also denser. Commercial yarns often have four plies, and there are also many multi-ply yarns with 10 or more singles plied together. Plies may be twisted together more or less tightly, and their direction may run parallel to the strand of yarn or in a circular twist around it. All these factors make the plies more or less visible, and the way they lie against each other will affect stitch definition. The degree and direction of twist also affects the look

and feel of the crocheted or knitted fabric, with loosely spun yarns producing a softer, loftier fabric, and tightly spun ones a more durable fabric that resists pilling.

One factor of particular significance to crochet is whether the yarns have been spun to the right or left, creating either an S- or a Z-twist. These names come from the direction of the diagonal stroke in the letter. In an S-twist, the plies slant from left to right; in a Z-twist, from right to left. Every "yarn over" in crochet twists the yarn once again, into a Z-twist if you're right-handed, or into an S-twist if you're a lefty. With lightly twisted yarns spun in the opposite direction of *your* twist, you may find the yarn tends to unwind and split as you work.

Although we work with plied yarns most often, mills are constantly designing new and interesting constructions that make yarns look and behave differently. The purpose is twofold: to arouse the insatiable appetites of yarn lovers with new looks and textures, and to make yarns more comfortable, practical, and durable.

An alternative to spun yarns is the **knitted tube**, a very fine yarn knitted into a tube with a hollow core. The resulting yarn is more light, airy, and elastic than its plied counterpart, and less likely to pill; examples of tube yarns can be found in animal, vegetable, and synthetics.

Thick/thin yarns are actually singles with pronounced variation in the size of the strand, making for a distinctive texture. **Bouclé** yarns are made by twisting two strands together at different tensions, one much tighter than the other, causing the looser strand to curl back around and create a distinct loop-covered texture.

Ribbon yarns are flat tape yarns usually woven from synthetics; they offer lovely color and shine. Many **novelty** yarns are made with several different fibers plied together, with yarn companies vying for the most interesting new blends and textures every season. Fibers vary greatly in how well they absorb dye, and you'll notice the difference in the intensity of colors from one yarn to the next.

Many classic yarns are offered in an enormous color range. Mixing and matching them is great fun. In recent years, **variegated** yarns with built-in color changes have attracted large followings. The color repeats in a variegated yarn may be regular or random, with abrupt color changes or subtle ones. Yarns can be **kettle dyed**, where all the colors are thrown into a pot with the yarn, or **space dyed**, where sections of yarn are dyed separately, each producing a distinct result. (No doubt techniques are being invented to produce an even greater variety of lovely color effects.) **Self-striping** sock yarns, which are hugely popular, are a clever example of variegation.

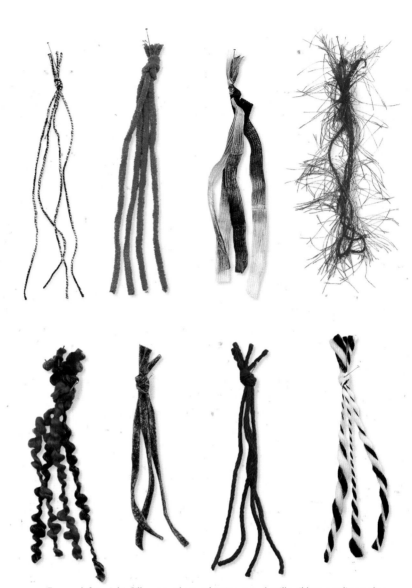

Top row left to right: Silk wrapped around cotton core, chenille, ribbon, acrylic novelty
Bottom row left to right: Bouclé, felt strip, medium weight cotton, chunky wool.

Yarn Weight

Probably the most significant factor in fabricology, besides fiber content, is the thickness of the yarn, which is referred to as its weight. The categories generally used—going from thinnest to bulkiest—are thread, lace weight, fingering, sport, double knitting (DK), worsted, bulky or chunky, and super bulky. The Craft Yarn Council has created a numbering system to label these categories. In this system, yarns are categorized by how many stitches are required to make 1 inch (2.5 cm) of knitted fabric. Because precise diameters aren't specified for any of these designations, you'll find a range of thicknesses within any category or number. This can lead to considerable confusion when substituting yarns in a pattern. Of the many weights available, DK and worsted weight are probably the most widely used, DK because it's thin enough to drape nicely in a garment, and worsted because it's an excellent weight for afghans.

Yarn Labels

If you're serious about crochet, learn to read yarn labels carefully. The yarn industry is well regulated and provides a great deal of important information on the label, including the exact percentage of fiber content. A 100% merino yarn will differ in softness, crispness, and springiness from one with a lower percentage. Some yarns contain blended fibers to keep the price tag down, but often fibers are blended to accentuate complementary qualities. The label will also inform you of the very important matter of yardage, crucial for calculating how many balls to buy. Furthermore, it tells you how to clean and care for your finished creation.

Yarn company websites are other great sources of information and will often explain what the company intended when it created a particular yarn. You won't find the construction method on a yarn label, but it's likely to be mentioned on the company's website.

As you begin to examine yarns more closely, your eye will distinguish between plied, tube, and tape yarns, and as you work with them, you'll learn how they tend to behave on the hook. Remember, though, nothing will give you as much information about a yarn as working with it directly on the hook.

Silk/stainless steel thread, wool/cashmere DK, wool bulky yarn

YARN WEIGHTS

The vast choice of yarns is a great boon for the contemporary crocheter. Learning to bring out the best in each yarn you encounter plays a major part in the mastery of fabricology. There's one simple rule of thumb to follow: in general, the more complex the yarn, the simpler the stitch best used to complement it. But be forewarned: this rule can be broken, and will be in this book!

 0 LACE — Fingering 10-count crochet thread

 1 SUPER FINE — Sock, Fingering, Baby

 2 FINE — Sport, Baby

 3 LIGHT — DK, Light Worsted

 4 MEDIUM — Worsted, Afghan, Aran

 5 BULKY — Chunky, Craft, Rug

 6 SUPER BULKY — Bulky, Roving

Source: Craft Yarn Council of America's www.YarnStandards.com

So Many Hooks to Choose From

When it comes to crochet hooks, size matters! The size of a crochet hook is measured in millimeters around its shaft, where the loop of the stitch sits. There are in-line hooks, where the head is the same width as the shaft, and others where the head is larger; hooks with and without a handgrip; and tapered hooks that are wider at the handle than the shaft. Hooks can be made of aluminum, bamboo, wood, and plastic, and the smaller hooks used for thread work are made of steel. The material out of which the hook is made affects its weight in the hand and also the fluidity factor—that is, whether the yarn moves smoothly on the hook. Bamboo hooks, for example, are incredibly light but a bit stickier with yarn than aluminum hooks.

Steel hooks are numbered from 00 to 14, with larger numbers indicating smaller hooks, as shown in the chart below right. Yarn hooks begin with letter B/1 (2.25mm) and go up to Q/19, a less commonly used hook that may be 15 or 16mm. For the most part, hook sizes are standardized internationally, but there are variations. For example, you can find hooks labeled "G" that are 4mm and others that are 4.5mm Older hooks manufactured before standardized sizing may have idiosyncratic measurements that fall in between today's sizes. Don't be afraid to use them, though; they can be useful for matching a particular gauge.

CROCHET HOOK SIZES

YARN HOOKS

US SIZE	METRIC
B-1	2.25 mm
C-2	2.75 mm
D-3	3.25 mm
E-4	3.50 mm
F-5	3.75 mm
G-6	4.00 mm
7	4.50 mm
H-8	5.00 mm
I-9	5.50 mm
J-10	6.00 mm
K-10 ½	6.50 mm
L-11	8.00 mm
M/N-13	9.00 mm
N/P-15	10.00 mm

STEEL HOOKS

US SIZE	METRIC
00	3.50 mm
0	3.25 mm
1	2.75 mm
2	2.25 mm
3	2.10 mm
4	2.00 mm
5	1.90 mm
6	1.80 mm
7	1.65 mm
8	1.50 mm
9	1.40 mm
10	1.30 mm
11	1.10 mm
12	1.00 mm
13	0.85 mm
14	0.75 mm

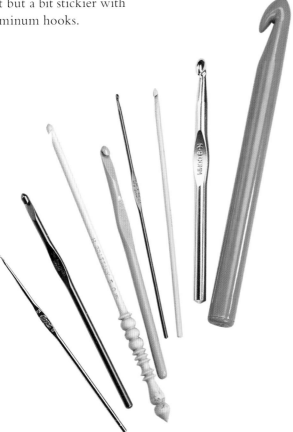

We all have our favorite hooks, either because they're pretty or easy to handle, or simply because we haven't tried any others. Having a variety of hooks in different shapes and materials is a great way to improve your crochet results. For example, some yarns such as mohair drag heavily on the hook and can tire hands and wrists or test your patience. A lightweight aluminum or bamboo hook can alleviate this problem. It's a matter of trial and error rather than one solution fits all.

Another significant factor is the shape if the hook itself—the "head" of the hook. Is it pointy, or rounded and bulbous? If you have a yarn that tends to split, go with a pointy hook, which works into stitches more easily.

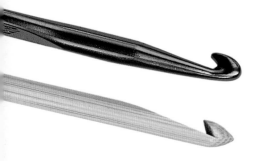

The construction of the hook, whether its head is rounded or angled or its shaft straight or tapered, will affect the way it handles yarn. Many people prefer one type of hook over another, or may switch depending on the yarn they're working. Hooks with grips are useful for stiffer yarns and can ease strain on the wrist and fingers. Because of subtle differences in how the hook moves with the fiber, you may not get the same gauge with the same-sized hook made of plastic or of metal, or one with a tapered shaft. In fact, if you're having difficulty matching the gauge of a particular pattern, changing the type of hook you're using (say, from a pointy-headed one to bulbous, or from metal to plastic) can subtly alter your gauge and solve this problem.

Most patterns prominently feature an admonition to check **gauge** before beginning, because crocheters differ dramatically in the tension they use. Gauge is a measure of how many stitches in 1 inch (2.5 cm). If you fail to match the gauge in a pattern, the finished item will be a different size. It's not a big deal if you're making a blanket or a throw, but it is if you're making a sweater! Because people work at different tensions, one person's F hook may be another's H. Gauge not only affects the finished size of your crochet, but also its drape. A loose gauge will yield a fluidity that's attractive in wearables, while a tight gauge provides more stiffness and structure.

The thinner the yarn being used, the smaller the hook, but any yarn can be worked with a range of hook sizes.

A good grasp of the tools and materials is the foundation for mastery of fabricology. I still have some yarns in my stash that looked lovely on the ball but never worked well for me on the hook. I purchased them before I understood the importance of yarn fibers, weight, and texture. In the chapters to come, I'll share the tips and techniques I've learned about these elements so that any yarn that comes your way can be swatched to perfection.

ariadne scarf

The Ariadne Scarf is a study in how different weights and fibers behave. It consists of the same medallion worked in a variety of yarns and gauges. By crocheting the same pattern in many kinds of yarns, you'll see the effect these variables have on results. Drape, a subject we'll examine more fully later, will vary considerably from one medallion to the next. The challenge is to increase the size of the medallions gradually, so you may have to experiment with different hook sizes. Fear not! It's a fun learning experience and an excellent exercise in exploring the relationship between yarn, hook, and stitches.

This project is a stash buster that will also teach you many things about how different yarns and hooks behave and interact. Go through your stash, starting with fine weights and working up gradually to bulky weights. Select colors and textures that blend or contrast nicely. It can be a challenge finding just the right yarns, but also lots of fun. If you can't find just the right color or weight to use, you can always mix two strands of yarns to come up with a desired color or thickness.

- You'll need approximately 50 feet (15.3 m) of yarn for a half-medallion, and double that for the full medallions at either end.

- The pattern begins with full medallions made of the finest weight yarns and works gradually up to heavier weights.

- Continue making half-medallions, selecting the next thickness of yarn and the appropriate hook that will make the size of the medallions grow gradually.

- Medallions on each half don't have to match exactly in size, as long as the gradation is fairly steady and gradual. You *do* want both last half-medallions to be fairly close in size.

- You don't have to stick to a sequence in which each yarn is thicker than the next, but can instead "cheat" a little on yarn weight to obtain a desired sequence of color by using a smaller hook with a slightly bulkier yarn. Experiment!

- I found it helpful to work both halves of the scarf at once. At times, I worked a medallion on one side and decided it belonged on the other.

- Examine the detail photos and yarn descriptions to see some of the variations I used. When you make your own version, you'll get hands-on lessons in fiber content and drape that will be invaluable in your study of fabricology.

Fingering weight, kid mohair, in kettle-dyed sea green, B/1 (2.25mm) hook
Sport weight, linen, in mocha, B/1 (2.25mm) hook
Fine weight, linen, in coral, C/2 (2.75mm) hook
Sport weight, viscose, in gold/brown, C/2 (2.75mm) hook
Sport weight, cotton/viscose, in variegated pastels, D/3 (3.25mm) hook
Worsted weight, cotton/rayon, in gold, D/3 (3.25mm) hook
Worsted weight, cotton/rayon, in variegated pastels, E/4 (3.50mm) hook
DK weight, cotton, in tomato, E/4 (3.50mm) hook

Worsted weight, acrylic, in two-tone teak/yellow, F/5 (3.75mm) hook
Bulky weight multi-strand, wool/acrylic, in variegated brown/orange, G/6, (4.00mm) hook
Bulky weight, wool, in variegated wheat/olive, H/8 (5.00mm) hook
Two strands, light worsted weight, linen/merino and mohair, in mango, G/6 (4.00mm) hook
Connecting medallion: bulky weight, ribbon, in variegated copper/grey G/6 (4.00) hook

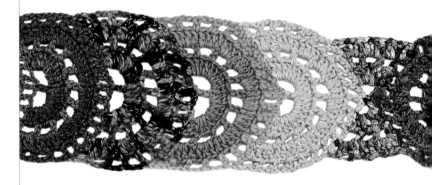

Fine weight, Shetland wool, in tomato, B/1 (2.25mm) hook
Fine weight, cotton, in lemon, B/1 (2.25mm) hook
Sport weight, cotton, in cantaloupe, B/1 (2.25mm) hook
Sport weight, cotton, in variegated orange/lime, C/2 (2.75mm) hook
Sport weight, mohair, in grapefruit, D/3 (3.25mm) hook
Sport weight, mohair, in chili red, D/3 (3.25mm) hook
Worsted weight, bouclé, in variegated lavender/orange, D/3 (3.25mm) hook

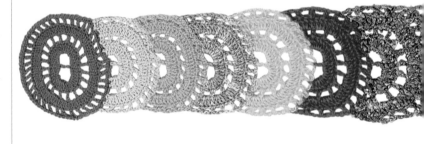

Worsted weight, linen in tangerine tweed, D/3 (3.25mm) hook
Yellow/gold, worsted weight cotton, C/2 (2.75mm) hook
Worsted weight, ribbon yarn, in variegated cream/brown, E/4 (3.50mm) hook
Two strands, worsted weight, wool blend and sport weight, mohair, in caramel/green, G/6 (4.00mm) hook
Bulky weight, multi-strand novelty, in green/brown, G/6 (4.00mm) hook

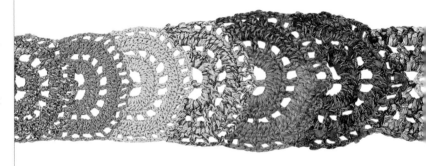

SKILL LEVEL: Easy

FINISHED MEASUREMENTS:
4–5'/1.25–1.5m in length

MATERIALS AND TOOLS
Approx 50yd/46m of 25 different yarns, ranging in thickness from fine to worsted weight; you may use fewer yarns and repeat some on either side

Range of crochet hooks from B/1 (2.25mm) to H/8 (5mm)

GAUGE
First full medallion = approx 3 x 3½"/8 x 9cm to 3½ x 4"/9 x 10cm depending on yarn used

Always take time to check your gauge.

SCARF HALF (MAKE 2)

FIRST FULL MEDALLION
With first color, ch 13.

RND 1: Dc in 9th ch to form first ring, ch 4, sk next 4 ch, sl st in last ch to form 2nd ring.

RND 2: Ch 3 (counts as dc), 9 dc in first ring, dc in ch at base of dc, 19 dc in next next ring, dc in next dc, 9 dc in other side of first ring, sl st to top of starting ch-3—40 dc.

RND 3: Ch 5 (counts as dc and ch 2), sk next dc, *dc in next dc, ch 2, sk next dc; rep from * around, ending with sl st into 3rd ch of starting ch-5—20 ch-2 spaces.

RND 4: Ch 3 (counts as dc), 3 dc in next ch-2 sp, *dc in next dc, 3 dc in next ch-2 sp; rep from * around, ending with sl st to top of tch—80 sts.

RND 5: Rep rnd 3—40 ch-2 sps.

RND 6: Ch 1, 2 sc in each ch-2 sp around, sl st in first sc to join, turn—80 sc. End off.

FIRST HALF-MEDALLION
With WS facing, join next color in 16th sc back from last sc on prev medallion. Row 1: Ch 1, sc in first sc, *ch 4, sk next 3 sc, dc in next sc, ch 4, sk next 3 sc, sc in next sc, ch 2, sk next sc, sl st to next sc, turn—2 ch-4 lps.

ROW 2: Ch 1, 9 dc in first ch-4 lp, dc in next dc, 9 dc in next ch-4 lp, sk next sc on first medallion, sl st to next sc, ch 2, sk next sc, sl st to next sc, turn—19 dc.

ROW 3: *Ch 2, sk next dc, dc in next dc, rep from * 8 times, ch 2, sk next sc on first medallion, sl st to next sc, ch 2, sk next sc, sl st to next sc, turn—10 ch-2 sps.

ROW 4: Ch 1, 3 dc in next ch-2 sp, *dc in next dc, 3 dc in ch-2 sp; rep from * 8 times, sk next sc on first medallion, sl st to next sc, ch 2, sk next sc, sl st to next sc, turn—39 dc.

ROW 5: *Ch 2, sk next dc, dc in next dc; rep from * 18 times, ch 2, sk next sc on first medallion, sl st to next sc—20 ch-2 sps. End off.

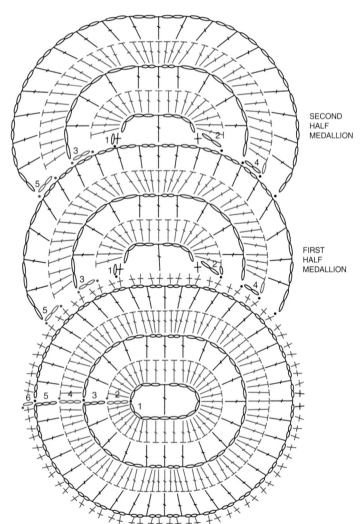

SECOND HALF MEDALLION

FIRST HALF MEDALLION

FIRST FULL MEDALLION

SECOND HALF-MEDALLION

Do not turn work. With WS facing, join next color in 8th dc from last st made on prev medallion (do not count ch 2 at beg as dc).

ROW 1: Ch 1, sc in first dc, ch 4, sk (ch-2 sp, dc, ch-2 sp), dc in next dc, ch 4, sk next (ch-2 sp, dc, ch-2 sp), sc in next dc, ch 2, sl st in next dc on prev medallion, turn—2 ch-4 lps.

ROW 2: Ch 1, 9 dc in first ch-4 lp, dc in next dc, 9 dc in next ch-4 lp, sl st in next dc on prev medallion, ch 2, sl st in next dc on prev medallion, turn—19 dc.

ROW 3: ★Ch 2, sk next dc, dc in next dc; rep from ★ 8 times, ch 2, sl st in next dc on prev medallion, turn—10 ch-2 sps.

ROW 4: Ch 1, 3 dc in ch-2 sp, ★dc in next dc, 3 dc in ch-2 sp; rep from ★ 18 times, sl st to next dc on prev medallion, ch 2, sl st to next dc on prev medallion, turn—39 dc.

ROW 5: ★Ch 2, sk next dc, dc in next dc; rep from ★ 18 times, ch 2, sl st to next dc on prev medallion—20 ch-2 sps. End off.

Following the instructions for Second Half-Medallion, work 9 additional half-medallions for each side of scarf, for a total of 11 half-medallions and one full medallion on each half.

CONNECTING MEDALLION
(TO CONNECT TWO HALVES OF SCARF)

The connecting medallion is made in two sections. Use the same yarn for both. The RS of scarf has solid dc rows showing fronts of stitches.

FIRST SECTION

Foundation Row: With RS of both halves facing up, work sl st through center dcs of last row on both halves, ch 2, sl st in next dc up on left half, turn. (**Note:** It must be on left half in order for RS of dc rows to face same direction as rest of work.)

ROW 1: Ch 3, sl st in next dc on opposite half, ch 2, sl st in next dc on same half, turn.

ROW 2: Ch 1, 7 dc in next ch-3 lp, sl st in next dc on opposite half, ch 2, sl st to next dc on same half, turn.

ROW 3: (Ch 2, sk next dc, dc in next dc) 3 times, ch 2, sl st to next dc on opposite half, ch 2, sl st to next dc on same half, turn—4 ch-2 sps.

ROW 4: Ch 1, (3 dc in next ch-2 sp, dc in next dc) 3 times, 3 dc in next ch-2 sp, sl st in next dc on opposite half—15 dc. End off.

SECOND SECTION

Turn work 180°. With WS facing, join yarn in first dc above sl st joining center dcs.

Rep rows 1–4 of First Section.

FINISHING

Gently steam connecting medallion and end medallions flat.

FIRST HALF

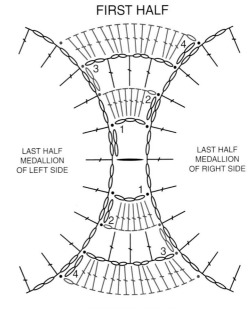

LAST HALF MEDALLION OF LEFT SIDE

LAST HALF MEDALLION OF RIGHT SIDE

SECOND HALF

CONNECTING MEDALLION

Designing Crochet Fabric

SINCE HUMANKIND LEARNED to spin fibers into string, fabrics have been woven and stitched. Even prehistoric fabrics were more than utilitarian. The makers explored color, texture, repeating patterns, and images as design elements added to their fabrics. Those aesthetic elements of fabric are as important in crochet as they are in any other textile.

In this context, it's useful to recall that crochet arose in Victorian times to produce lace—a much-prized fabric of the time. Prior to the early nineteenth century, lace was made with needles and bobbins, and was tremendously labor- and time-intensive. Crochet accomplished the same task in a fraction of the time.

In lacework, a decorative pattern is created by arranging stitches into images, and surrounding these images with open space or simple lines. To achieve this with crochet, very thin threads composed of stiff fibers such as cotton and linen were used. These sturdy fibers created crisp designs that were clearly visible to the eye. The heavier yarns of today, coupled with contemporary tastes in fashion, invite us to explore new and innovative ways to design crochet fabric.

Stitch patterns for swatches marked with
can be found starting on page 120.

Crochet stitches provide a strong visual element to our fabric. Even simple stitches do not look plain, because we can see the parallel lines of individual stitches, and the wrapping of yarn on taller stitches. Every stitch pattern plays with this visual element in some way, giving us many choices in the surface we want to create.

Remember, however, that for stitch patterns to be clear to the eye, they must present clean lines and spaces. Some yarns with variegated colors, highly textured surfaces like bouclé, or multistranded yarns will obscure this clarity. Learning to see and work with the interaction between yarn and stitches is central to fabricology.

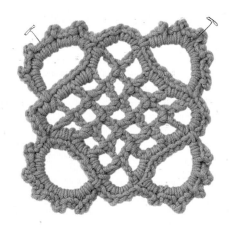

Traditional lacework motifs

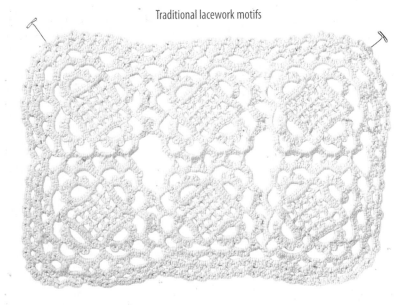

The Crochet Stitch

The crochet stitch is a fascinating animal—because it depends on looping and twisting yarn, it's bulky by nature. Of course, in the early days of crochet, the tiniest threads were used, and bulky stitches were not an issue. But the days of blindingly tiny crochet work is long gone, and today many of the yarns we use present puzzles precisely because of the amplification of yarn, and, consequently, the stitch.

Stitch Definition

What is a well-defined crochet stitch? It's when each stitch stands out in the fabric, and the structure of the stitch is apparent. In a well-defined crochet stitch, you can see the individual strands of yarn, and the wrapping and looping of one strand around another.

Historically, as yarn has grown larger, the stitches have become more pronounced. In later twentieth-century crochet and worsted weight yarns, the stitches are very prominent. This assertive quality of large crochet stitches can be more eye-catching than knit stitches. A knit stitch consists of one loop linked to the next, making a relatively small stitch and uniform-looking fabric. Knitted fabric, unless adorned with cables or other more complex stitch patterns, is usually perceived as plain fabric. Crochet stitches have several more wraps of yarn per stitch than knit stitches do. Crochet stitches can also be created in various heights—the taller the stitch, the more "yarn overs" to make them. Every yarn over in crochet is visible on the post of the stitch, and all of this makes for a more intricate pattern of stitches. The upshot is, crochet just doesn't look like plain fabric, even when we do rows of simple stitches without height variation.

The strong definition of crochet stitches can be an asset that makes stitch patterns crisp and beautiful. On the other hand, there are instances where it's preferable to minimize the stitch definition. This can be accomplished with fuzzy or very soft yarns. Variegated yarns can also obscure stitch definition.

What the crochet stitch may lack in delicacy, it makes up for in many other ways. Knitted stitches must always be done in rows; crochet stitches have more structural integrity. They can latch on to one another at any point, in any direction, all bunched together into a small space or set apart with only chains between the stitches. It's this architectural quality that gives crochet its marvelous ability to create shapes and patterns. I call this *crochet graphics*, and it's a very important factor in the mastery of essential tools (see page 44).

Stitch definition is an important variable we can use in creating crochet fabric. Each yarn lends its own characteristic look to crochet stitches, and you can't always tell from looking at the ball: you have to stitch it to see it. Some yarns show each stitch with great clarity, and others blur them. Either way, we can create interesting fabrics, as long as we consider this element in our planning.

When stitch definition is absent, it's useful to have other ways to give visual definition to crochet fabric. One way to do this is to use well-defined stitch patterns. The essence of every stitch pattern is a repeating visual of some kind, and so you need to select a yarn that allows that visual to come through. Some stitch patterns are defined by grouping stitches together, forming shapes such as fans or shells. These shapes stand out well in the fabric, because we can see the stitches moving in various directions. Even more obvious to the eye are open work stitch patterns, where the shapes are surrounded by air. Stitch patterns are one of the great resources crochet has at its disposal, and they come in so many guises that there's one to suit almost any yarn you can imagine.

Crochet vs. knit

Working with and without Stitch Definition

We've all seen how some yarns offer more stitch definition than others. Obviously, using a smooth yarn makes a more defined stitch than one made with textured yarn. Another quality that affects stitch definition is the stiffness of the fiber—cotton or linen yarns, for example, provide very well-defined stitches.

Stitch definition can also be enhanced by how the yarn reflects light, with lighter colors giving stronger stitch definition. Plied yarns have a subtle dimensionality that heightens stitch definition, as does the shimmer in some yarns. A firm, bouncy yarn will form and hold the shape of the stitch well. With softer yarns, the stitches may not be as well defined, but ply and shimmer can make up for what's lost.

Here are several swatches using different fibers and yarns, all in the same stitch pattern—a favorite we've all seen many times—fans alternating with single crochet stitches, interlocking in alternate rows to create a closed fabric. Let's examine how stitch definition, or its absence, works in these samples.

- The turquoise swatch is made with a crisp, shiny, sport weight silk, and each stitch is clearly defined. Not only are individual stitches obvious, but also the fan pattern is clear. Notice how smooth, thin yarn with sheen makes a clean, attractive stitch with strong pattern definition.

- In the angora yarn sample, the fuzz decreases stitch definition, but individual stitches are still clear, as is the shell pattern swatch. The overall effect is softer, both visually and to the touch, than the silk swatch.

- In the third swatch, there's not much of anything to see except lots of fuzz. This soft synthetic yarn is lovely to feel, but in a well-balanced swatch, I like to see some evidence of the stitches and pattern.

Sport weight silk

Angora

Synthetic Yarn

The movement and direction of stitches is another important element in working with yarns and stitch patterns. Let's look at one more swatch with the same shell pattern used earlier, this time in a variegated ribbon yarn.

This result surprised me, as yarns often do. My expectation was that it would result in a knotty blur, yet there's just enough definition supplied by the fans. Ribbon yarns can be very tricky, because the flat, wide shape of the strand makes each stitch look a little different, depending on the way the yarn lies or curls. That, in turn, can interfere with the clarity of stitch patterns. The fact that this yarn is variegated also blurs definition, because color changes can interfere with the clarity of a pattern.

So what makes this swatch work? I think it has to do with the construction of the fan shape—stitches are moving in different directions, which gives the eye something to follow, and helps us see each stitch more clearly.

What can be done when the yarn tends to fight definition? I think of this as a matter of imposing visual definition where there is none. If the swatch I'm making looks like a blur, I try to figure out ways of adding a repeating visual element.

The blue and white swatch below demonstrates how color and a big bold stitch pattern (Catherine's Diamond, in this case) can impose structure and create a strong visual in a fuzzy yarn.

More Ways to Define Crochet Fabric

Another way to add definition to crochet is by using a pattern where the stitches don't lie absolutely flat, but rather "pop out" from the fabric. It's the nature of crochet that dimension is often added, because groups of stitches tend to bulk up. Even the fan pattern we've been looking at does it a bit. Bobbles and puff stitches create obvious dimension in our crochet fabric.

This pattern, which I call Little Leaves, consists of one single crochet and two double crochet stitches worked in the same stitch, skipping two stitches, and then repeating. This stitch combination produces a leaf-shaped cluster, and the shorter stitch tends to squeeze its taller companion a bit, causing the slight raising of the pattern.

Just to compare, I've used the same stitch pattern with four different yarns: a crisp worsted weight cotton with lots of stitch definition, a soft worsted weight wool, a wool/acrylic blend thick/thin yarn that's somewhere between worsted and chunky weight, and a mohair. It's clear that each of these yarns has different degrees of stitch definition, with the cotton being the most defined, the wool/acrylic showing the

Shell pattern in ribbon yarn

Color and bold pattern impose structure

Worsted weight cotton

Worsted weight wool

Wool/acrylic blend

Synthetic yarn

least definition, and the wool falling somewhere in between. In each case, however, the dimension that the stitch pattern provides adds visual structure. Another reason the stitch pattern is clear, regardless of stitch definition, is that each "little leaf" is made on an angle, so strands of yarn move in different directions, making them more visible to the eye.

You can see how this added dimension affects the super fuzzy synthetic yarn we looked at earlier. I think it's an improvement. Just a small degree of dimensional definition turns a fuzzy blur into a pleasing design.

At right are more examples of a closed stitch pattern with two yarns of varying weights, fibers, and stitch definition. Closed stitch patterns are the opposite of open work or lacy patterns—in other words, they make a continuous fabric, not one with holes.

One swatch is a lilac DK weight bamboo yarn with strong stitch definition; the other is a mohair where fuzz obscures the individual stitches. This closed stitch pattern is quite intricate, with stitches moving in several directions—what I call "multidirectional stitches." The clustering of stitches also adds dimension. Both of these qualities are heightened in the bamboo swatch and minimized in the mohair.

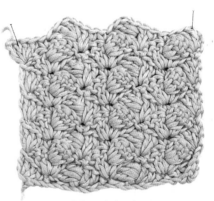

DK weight bamboo

Mohair

Are you starting to see how various elements of crochet can be controlled and manipulated? So far we've discussed stitch definition and it's absence, and two ways to add visual structure: multidirectional stitch patterns and patterns that add dimension. There are many more ways, of course, and we'll get to those!

The stitch pattern shown below has a lot going on, doesn't it? It consists of a row of bobbles alternating with a row of crossed stitches. The bobble is a cluster of stitches that, even more than Little Leaves, adds dimension to the surface—the more stitches in your bobble, the more it will puff up. In between each bobble is a space, which allows you to see the individual bobbles. The crossed stitches also bulk up and add dimension, and are surrounded by space that helps them stand out. What we have, then, is an interesting, complex surface that includes dimensional stitches and open work. How does this stitch pattern interact with the three yarns shown here?

- The worsted weight light pink merino has a tight twist in the yarn; the stitches really pop, but it's almost overkill with so much going on. With the strong stitch definition in this yarn, I'd probably choose a simpler stitch pattern, and one with less dimension.

- The sport weight silk works very nicely, and the shimmer of the silk adds attractive luster. It may be the scale of the stitches that makes it more pleasing than the worsted weight swatch, although this is a matter of individual taste.

- Look at how interesting the ribbon yarn swatch turned out! The dimension of the crossed stitches is minimized because the yarn lies flatter,

but the space around the bobbles provides clean lines, making it easy to see. To me, this is a good use of a variegated ribbon yarn, where the challenge is to provide more visual definition without adding too much bulk.

Here are two swatches with a lacy pattern. The first uses a DK weight wool with strong definition, and the other is in a medium weight mohair with far less definition. I would imagine that a pattern like this was first designed on much thinner threads. To my eye, when blown up in heavier weight yarns, the individual stitches begin to fight with the images of petals and picots. For this reason, I like it better in the mohair, where the stitch definition is lessened dramatically.

Bobbles alternating with crossed stitches

Lacy patterns

More Dimensional Effects

Crochet offers many great ways to create dimensional effects in fabric. A popular example of this is the post stitch, which is worked around the post of the stitch below instead of into the top of the stitch, as is normally done. An almost limitless number of stitch patterns have been created using post stitches, such as the one in the following three samples.

As before, I've worked the same stitch in yarns that have varying degrees of stitch definition. The yarn with linen content shows the most stitch definition, the mohair blend shows the least, and the wool/acrylic blend is somewhere in between. The dimensional post stitches lend visual structure to all three, yet the overall effect of each swatch is very different.

The zigzag post swatch made with worsted weight wool using two different dimensional stitches: double crochet post stitches and back loop single crochet stitches. In each row, the two post stitches are moved over one stitch, creating a zigzag effect, while the back loop stitches form a horizontal line.

A similar complex post stitch pattern is basketweave stitch, which is used in the Papagena's Pouch on page 39. It's done in worsted weight cotton, a fiber that lends strong stitch definition and creates a very crisp and clear dimensional effect. Dimensional stitches tend to bulk up the fabric, making them heavier and stiffer, which is perfect for a bag, but not as suitable for an item of clothing.

At far right is a more dimensional effect that's less common than post stitches: in this pattern, a series of stitches of graduated heights is worked around the posts of two adjacent double crochets, resulting in a petal-like protrusion. I used a shiny wool/rayon blend and a mohair, which resulted in very different degrees of stitch definition. I love both looks, and am pondering ways they can be used in designs.

Linen

Zigzag post

Wool/acrylic blend

Petal-like protrusions

Mohair blend

Loop Stitches

Stitch patterns that add dimension to the fabric will supply visual definition to almost any yarn, and that makes them very useful. If you are after a very strong and clear dimensional look, as in crochet cables, choose a yarn that has lots of stitch definition, such as linen or cotton. Subtler effects made with less defined yarns can also be very attractive. Keep in mind that all dimensional stitches will also add bulk to the fabric, which may detract from drape. (See page 32.)

Unique fabrics can be created by using loop stitches of various kinds. For an extreme dimensional effect, stitches called fur or Astrakhan can be found in many stitch dictionaries. Below are two swatches, one in a single color and one with furry stripes. This fake fur is often used as a trim for gloves, hats, and jackets, and is a fun tool for designing unique garments. The furry effect is created by

making many loops of chain stitches and placing them close together so that the plain fabric underneath is obscured.

Another type of loop stitch is made with single strands, not chains. Long loops like this are more fluid. In the swatch pictured below, I added three rows of sc between the loop rows to allow the loops to lay flat.

Long loops with plain rows

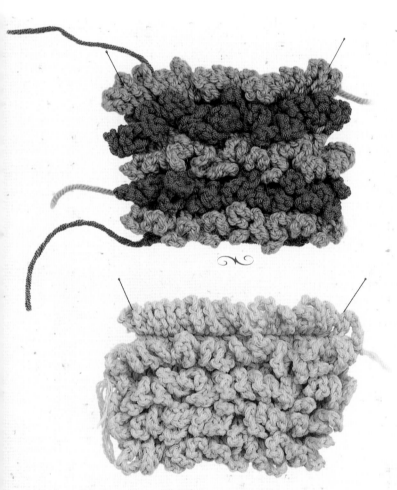

Astrakhan or fur stitch

Perhaps my favorite loop stitch of all is Solomon's Knot, a stitch made with very long loops discretely gathered by single crochet stitches. This technique allows us to see individual strands of yarn unadorned, and for that reason it's fantastic for novelty yarns, such as those used in the following samples. Fabric made using Solomon's Knot offers great possibilities for a scarf or shawl, and I'd like to see it used to create a curtain, too.

• One swatch uses a novelty yarn that would pose quite a challenge with normal crochet stitches.

• Another swatch is a silk with lots of texture and variation in width.

In the Solomon's Knot stitch, the knots form a diamond shape. Because the loops are loose and without much tension, the diamond shape is not strongly defined; however, when worked up, it will vary depending on what yarn is used.

Recently I found a rare variation of Solomon's Knot in an old stitch dictionary. It's shown below in two different yarns: a worsted weight cotton and a fingering weight textured yarn. There's more visual definition here than with plain Solomon's Knot, because the puffs are a clear repeating element. Although traditional Solomon's Knot creates drape, this variation is less so, because it includes the bulky little puff stitch. Still, it has sufficient drape for a wearable and would make a fine lacy shawl or evening jacket.

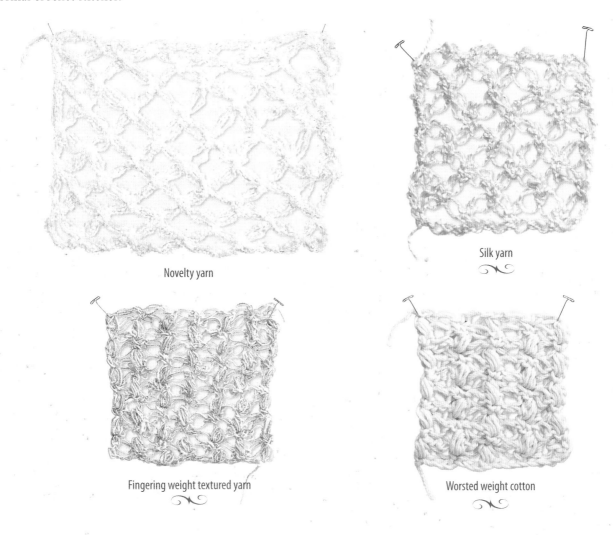

Novelty yarn

Silk yarn

Fingering weight textured yarn

Worsted weight cotton

Drape versus Structure

No doubt you've noticed my frequent references to the quality of drape. Drape is one of the primary properties of fabric, and its opposite is stiffness. Depending on what you need the fabric to do, you will want more or less of one or the other. If you've made a lovely afghan with worsted weight yarn, have you ever draped it around your body to see what it would look like to wear? Most likely, it would be better suited for a heavy cardigan or jacket, where you would want similar thickness in the fabric. On the other hand, if you want a soft indoor sweater, you probably want a fabric that has more drape than afghan fabric typically does.

Drape is one of those qualities that is hard to define, but we see it in all kinds of fabric, from a skirt to curtains to clerical robes. A fabric that drapes is loose enough to flow around the body and move with it in a graceful way. This is one of the more difficult qualities to achieve in crochet, because of the inherent bulkiness of the crochet stitch. Fortunately, with the fabulous new yarns of today, and the myriad stitch patterns at our disposal, it can be done. To give a worsted weight yarn more drape, try an open lacy stitch pattern, or use a larger hook, and you'll have it. Try a finer weight yarn and you'll get even more.

Worsted weight yarns are great for afghans, but when you challenge yourself to do something else with crochet, such as a sweater, jacket, vest, skirt, purse, or hat, you may find other weights of yarn will improve your result. For a heavy-duty item such as a rug, a bulky yarn can get you there much faster; for a wearable, a DK or sport weight may yield a much more pleasing result.

If you've ever made a crocheted hat, you've probably faced the issue of drape. You might want a hat that's very structured and holds its shape well, or one that's looser and molds to the head.

Although the yarns used in the two hats shown here are similar (a bouclé mohair), the density of the stitch pattern and the size of the hook make a difference in the degree of drape or structure in the hat. Let's look more closely at how to control this element in our crochet.

Drape vs. structure

Fiber Content and Drape

If you're hoping for a simple solution, take a deep breath; the truth is, obtaining great results with drape is one of the most challenging aspects of crochet. As mentioned, the weight and fiber of the yarn must be considered. Bulkier yarns, as a rule, are less suited for drape than thinner ones. But two yarns of the same weight will vary depending upon the stiffness of the fibers used.

- Although all yarns are different depending on how they are manufactured, it's safe to say that fibers with more stiffness include cotton, linen, and hemp.

- In the animal family, alpaca, fine merinos, and mohair provide more drape than other less costly wools.

- Silk can drape marvelously, but less expensive silks can be quite stiff.

- Some acrylic and synthetic blends have been designed with the quality of drape in mind, and creative swatching will reveal the degree of drape (see page 70).

In general, manufacturing a yarn for drape means using more costly materials and time-intensive processes, thereby increasing its price.

Hook Size and Drape

Next in importance with regard to the drape factor is the hook size you choose. Let's look at two swatches worked with a worsted weight merino in the same stitch pattern, an open work fan.

- With a C hook, the fabric is dense, tight, and quite thick—just the thing for a sturdy scarf or cardigan.

- With a much larger hook—an I hook in this case—the result is more drape, creating a soft fabric suitable for a vest or shawl.

Which hook would you normally use with worsted weight yarn? My hunch is that it would be one of the hook sizes that falls between these two examples. I purposely chose more extreme hooks to illustrate the greater choice they can give you.

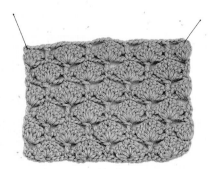

C hook

I hook

Stitch Pattern and Drape

One of the most important factors that can influence drape is the density of the stitch pattern—that is, whether there is space or "air" in the pattern, and how large the spaces are.

- Taller stitches result in more drape than shorter stitches by virtue of the separation between them.

- Clustered stitches are stiffer, because they cram many strands into one place and thicken the fabric.

- Textured stitches, whether post or spike stitches, or dimensional stitches such as bobbles and puffs, also add density and thickness to the fabric.

Degree of Drape
for Various Items

It's wise to determine the type of fabric most appropriate for the project you're making, being mindful of the stiffness/drape issue. You can achieve the lightest, airiest fabric for a summer top, a comfortable coziness for an indoor sweater, a woven, tailored feel for a blazer, or a chill-busting heavy-duty coat. For pieces such as hats and bags, you can provide as much structure as needed to hold the item's shape and improve its functionality.

If we construct a continuum that begins with structure at one end and drape on the other, we can place various items along it. On the structured end would be crochet sculpture, such as amigurumi, dolls, and jewelry. Next, you'd have items such as bags, then hats, then coats and jackets. Further along, on the drape end, you'd find scarves and ponchos. Cardigans and indoor sweaters need considerable drape, and summer wear perhaps even more than winter wear. Possibly a shawl should be fashioned with the most drape, because it is meant to fall gracefully around the neck and shoulders.

Our study of fabricology began with an understanding of the three basic tools of crochet, and builds with an understanding of the elements for designing a pleasing visual surface. We've explored how different elements—stitch definition, visual definition, dimensional effects, stitch patterns, drape, and structure—add to our knowledge about the fabrics we make. No matter what your level of crochet skills, observing the smaller components of crochet and understanding how they interact, allows you to create a lovely, functional fabric with almost any yarn. Learning to see how the various stitches and techniques work with individual yarns and their characteristics is key to crochet fabricology.

Guidelines for Drape/Structure

To summarize, here are important considerations regarding yarn, hook size, and stitch pattern that affect drape or thickness in fabric:

To add drape to your fabric you can use:	To add more density and structure to your fabric you can use:
Soft yarn	Heavier yarn
Thin yarn	Textured yarn
Larger hooks	Stiffer fiber
Less dense stitch patterns	Smaller hooks
More spaces between stitches	Shorter stitches
Taller stitches	Closed, dense stitch patterns
	Dimensional stitches, such as post stitches, spikes, bobbles, and popcorns

rusalka wrap

The Rusalka Wrap is made with a variegated sock yarn, where color repeats are quite short. The color changes in a yarn of this type tend to interfere with both stitch definition and pattern definition. Yarn lovers often complain of "pooling"—blobs of color—and other blurry effects of variegated yarn. Adding more visual structure when working with variegated yarns will cure these ills—the challenge is to find a pattern that can hold its own despite the color changes. The wavy line created by ripple patterns is certainly a visual feature that adds definition, but with this yarn, it wasn't quite enough.

To increase the pattern's visibility, I found a ripple pattern with open spaces, which makes the individual stitches, and the ripple effect, more apparent.

Then, I outlined the ripple pattern with a row of single crochet worked a special way to create a strong line of dimension along each ripple. The end result is a clearly defined ripple that forms a wavy line, creating a lovely counterpoint to the color changes in the yarn. To my eye, it's the best of both worlds, the impressionistic dappling of color within a clearly structured frame. Because this is made with a thin yarn, and makes use of open work, it drapes very nicely.

SKILL LEVEL: Intermediate

FINISHED MEASUREMENTS
Approx 10 x 71"/25.5 x 180.5cm

MATERIALS AND TOOLS
1148 yd/105m size sock weight 【1】 superwash merino wool/bamboo blend yarn in variegated blue/green/white

C/2 (2.75mm) hook or size needed to obtain gauge

Yarn needle

GAUGE
1 patt rep = approx 2½"/6.5cm; 6 rows in patt = approx 2"/5cm

Always take time to check your gauge.

SPECIAL ABBREVIATIONS
Special front post sc (SFPsc): Insert hook from back to front in first tr, complete sc (first SFPsc made); ★insert hook from front to back in same tr, then insert hook from back to front in next tr, complete sc (SFPsc made); rep from ★ for each additional SFPsc.

PATTERN STITCHES

RIPPLE PATTERN
Note: There will be two skipped sts at the bottom "dip" of each ripple.

Ch a multiple of 18 plus 4.

ROW 1: 4 tr in 5th ch from hook, ★(tr in next ch, sk next ch) 4 times, (sk next ch, tr in next ch) 4 times★★, 5 tr in ea of next 2 ch; rep from ★ across, ending last rep at ★★, 5 tr in last ch, turn.

ROW 2: Ch 1, SFPsc in ea st across, turn.

ROW 3: Ch 4 (counts as tr), 4 tr in first st, ★(tr in next st, sk next st) 4 times, (sk next st, tr in next st) 4 times★★, 5 tr in ea of next 2 sts; rep from ★ across, ending last rep at ★★, 5 dc in last st, turn.

Rep rows 2 and 3 for patt.

WRAP

Ch 486 plus 4.

ROWS 1–3: Work in Ripple patt on 27 patt reps.

ROWS 4–29: Rep rows 2 and 3.

LAST ROW: Ch 1, sc in ea st across. End off.

EDGING

With RS facing, working into base of foundation ch, tie on yarn in first ch, ch 1, sc evenly across, working 1 sc in ch at base of ea tr, 1 sc in each ch-1 sp, and 2 sc in ea ch-2 sp. End off. Weave in ends with yarn needle.

FINISHING

Steam block work to flatten and open up lacework.

This project was crocheted with:
3 skeins UrbanGypZ Artisan Superwash Bamboo Blend Sock Yarn, fingering weight (**1**), 65% superwash merino wool, 35% bamboo, 4oz/113g = 560yd/512m, in Earth Day

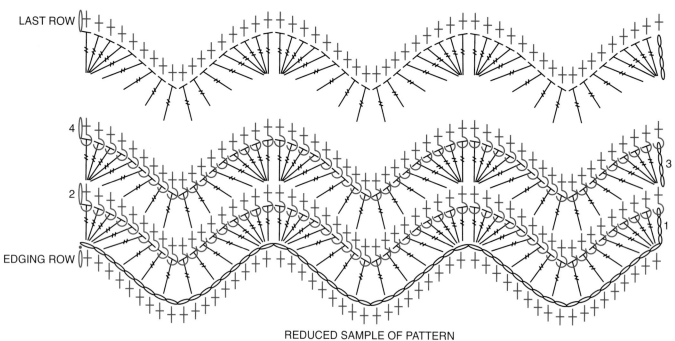

REDUCED SAMPLE OF PATTERN

papagena's pouch

Papagena's Pouch uses
a favorite post stitch pattern
called basketweave. I find this
pattern is best worked in a yarn
with strong stitch definition. The
worsted weight cotton provides
just that. Because it's a dimensional stitch that adds bulk, the
fabric is structured rather than
drapey, and that's a good thing
for a bag. The bag will hold
its shape better and be more
durable. The project would
look fine in just one color, but I
couldn't resist adding an additional visual element of colored
stripes. This organic yarn comes
in natural muted colors, so
the stripes are nice and subtle.
Because the overall effect of the
fabric is understated, I added a
contemporary strap to give it
some visual punch.

SKILL LEVEL: Easy

FINISHED MEASUREMENTS

11"/28cm wide x 12"/30.5cm deep

Back/flap piece 11"/28cm wide x 18"/45.5cm long

Front piece 11"/28cm wide x 11"28/cm long

MATERIALS AND TOOLS

Color A: 164yd/150m worsted weight 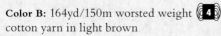 cotton yarn in cream

Color B: 164yd/150m worsted weight cotton yarn in light brown

G/6 (4 mm) hook or size to obtain gauge

Yarn needle

½ yd/0.5m of 45"/114.5cm-wide fabric of your choice for lining bag

Sewing needle

Thread

Pins

Approx 1yd/1m of 1¾"/4.5cm-wide plastic chain, plus 3 extra chains (optional)

GAUGE

16 sts = 4¼"/11cm; 6 rows = 2½"/6.5cm

Always take time to check your gauge.

SPECIAL ABBREVIATIONS

Front Post Double Crochet (FPdc): Yo, insert hook from front to back to front again around the post of the st below, complete dc as usual.

Back Post Double Crochet (BPdc): Yo, insert hook from back to front to back again around the post of the st below, complete dc as usual.

PATTERN STITCHES

BASKETWEAVE STITCH

Ch a multiple of 8 plus 5, plus 2 for tch.

ROW 1: Dc in 3rd ch from hook and in ea ch across.

ROW 2: Ch 2 (counts as dc), FPdc in ea of next 4 dc, ★BPdc in ea of next 4 dc, FPdc in ea of next 4 dc; rep from ★ across, ending with dc in top of tch, turn.

ROW 3: Ch 2 (counts as dc), BPdc in ea of next 4 dc, ★FPdc in ea of next 4 dc, BPdc in ea of next 4 dc; rep from ★ across, ending with dc in top of tch, turn.

ROW 4: Rep row 3.

ROW 5: Rep row 2.

ROW 6: Rep row 3.

ROW 7: Rep row 3.

Rep rows 2–7 for patt.

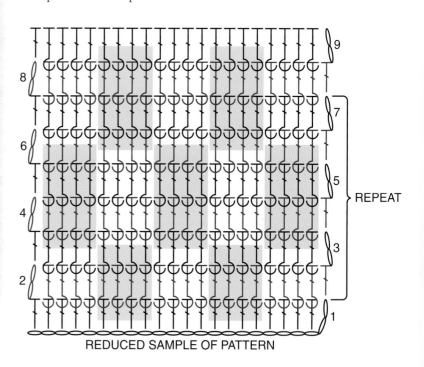

REDUCED SAMPLE OF PATTERN

REVERSE SINGLE CROCHET (RSC)

Working in opposite direction from how you normally work (left to right if you are right-handed, right to left if you are left-handed), insert hook in next st, draw lp through st and under lps on hook, yo, draw lp through 2 lps on hook.

BACK/FLAP PIECE

Starting at side edge, with A, ch 71.

Work in basketweave stitch on 70 sts, in the following color sequence: 6 rows of A; 3 rows of B; 3 rows of A; 3 rows of B; 3 rows of A; 3 rows of B; 6 rows of A.

FRONT

With B, ch 47.

Work in basketweave stitch on 46 sts, in the following color sequence: 6 rows of A; 3 rows of B; 3 rows of A; 3 rows of B; 3 rows of A; 3 rows of B; 6 rows of A.

FINISHING

Weave in all ends with yarn needle. Steam block pieces lightly to square off any unevenness in fabric. Place WS of both pieces together with left side edge of front aligned with left side edge of bottom. Starting at top right corner of front piece, and with RS facing, tie on B, ch 1. Picking up one strand from front and back of bag, work RSC around side edge, bottom, and opposite side edge of front; with same strand, sl st evenly across top edge of front to tighten. End off.

BAG LINING

Measure and cut the lining fabric ½"/1.3cm wider than the width of the bag and double the length of the bag pocket plus 2"/5cm. Fold the lining in half crosswise. Sew both side seams using ⅜"/1cm seam allowance. Trim the side seams. Fold the top of the lining pocket down 1"/2.5cm to outside of lining. Pin and sew along the top edge of the fold.

BAG TABS (TO CONNECT HANDLE TO BAG)

Measure and cut one tab 12"/30.5cm long and 2"/5cm wide. Fold in half lengthwise and press. Open the tab, fold both edges toward the center, and press. Fold the tab in half crosswise and sew along both side edges of the tab. Cut the tab in half, forming two tabs; loop one tab around the plastic chain at end of handle and sew folded tab to side seams securely. Sew other tab on opposite side of bag.

Place and pin lining inside the pocket, and hand sew lining in place around top edge.

Optional: Using matching thread, sew 3 additional plastic chains to front fold of bag as shown.

This project was crocheted with:
Lion Brand Yarn's Organic Cotton, worsted weight yarn, 100% organic cotton, 1.75oz/50g = 82yd/75m

(A) 2 skeins, Almond (002)

(B) 2 skeins, Bark (003)

How Stitch Patterns Work

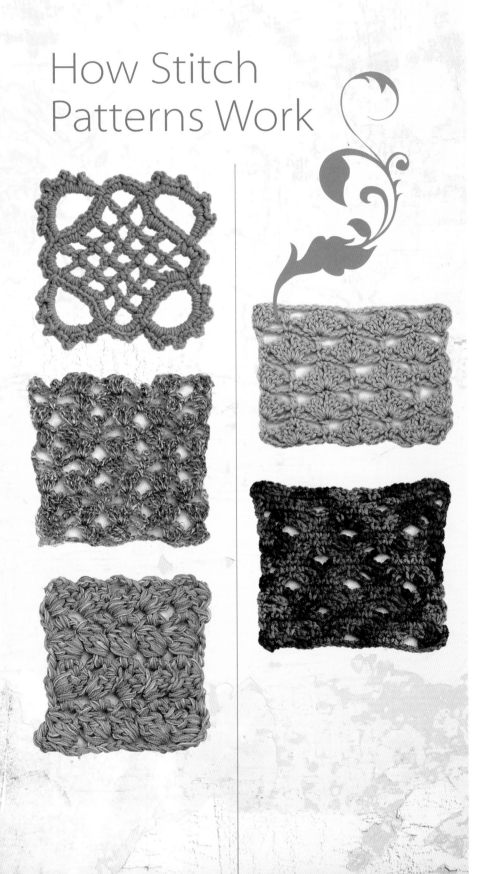

MANY OF THE SURFACES we see around us use the elements out of which they are constructed to create designs or patterns. Beautiful parquet floors are made by arranging wood slats in patterns. Similarly, baskets are woven with reeds of different thicknesses and a great variety of patterns. Both of these surfaces share elements with crochet, because they are composed of individual units arranged in recognizable patterns. In crochet, naturally, the individual units are the stitches.

In the previous chapter we began to explore crochet's most remarkable resource—the infinite variety of stitch patterns the craft has generated. Some patterns are all about bold drama, while others are more delicate and intricate. Some are geometric; others feature recognizable shapes such as fans and shells. These characteristics, as well as the size and scale of the pattern, are very important elements in our exploration of crocheted fabric.

Stitch patterns for swatches marked with
can be found starting on page 120.

What Are Crochet Graphics?

To get a better handle on analyzing stitch patterns, I've come up with the term crochet graphics. I'm interested in how visual elements in crochet work, how patterns are created, and how they are perceived. There are two broad categories of stitch patterns—closed or open work—and there are many variations of both. Crochet uses a variety of effects alone or in combination to achieve discernible shapes and repeating patterns.

- Grouping stitches in clusters, fans, shells, or other shapes.

- Bulking stitches together to create puffs or bobbles.

- Using post stitches to create linear patterns.

- Mixing stitches of different heights together in a row.

- Alternating open and closed areas to create an image, as in filet crochet.

When you analyze a stitch pattern that you want to work with consider also the question of its scale. All stitch patterns require some type of repeat; how many stitches and rows the pattern requires will tell you the scale of the pattern. Smaller patterns are usually more subtle and textural; larger, more intricate patterns create a busier or bolder surface. And between these two extremes there is every imaginable variety of scale.

The two swatches below have bold geometric shapes that are clearly defined by the space around them.

The fan pattern is offset by a row of double crochet mesh; the squares are outlined with chain stitches in crisscrossing lines.

On the next page are two examples worked in a linen blend DK yarn, one with a bolder pattern than the other.

- The more muted example shows double crochet stitches that form V shapes, but nothing solid emerges into a clear shape. It's more of a visual texture than a series of recognizable images.

- The other sample has a fan repeated over several rows, with plenty of open space around it, so the shapes stand out in strong definition

Depending on the type of visual surface you prefer, and other design elements in your fabric, you might choose one over the other. Each has its place, and sometimes the more muted effect is the right one.

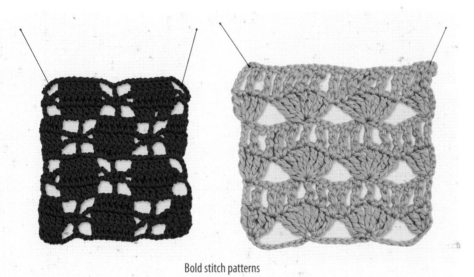

Bold stitch patterns

When we move from the delicate small threads of the past to the larger yarns of today, we dramatically alter the scale of stitch patterns. At the bottom of the page are two swatches of a traditional lacy stitch pattern combining bobbles, picots, and chains. What a difference the yarn makes! On the orange, the white inner strand lends strong definition, but it is softened by the orange. Using a much finer variegated yarn, the pattern is far less visible, but

there's an overall impressionistic effect that's appealing.

Below right are two scarf swatches, one with delicate filet and shells, and the other with a simpler but more emphatic stitch pattern. The first swatch is lovely in a traditional way; the second, in my view, is a new and attractive take on crochet lace.

• In the first, worked with fine weight yarn, mesh is used to create

a "plain" background from which the shell groups emerge. The fine weight yarn preserves the delicacy of chain mesh, which might look ungainly in heavier yarn.

• In the second, the yarn has lots of character and visual complexity, due to surface and thickness variations. The clean, straightforward stitch pattern complements the yarn, and the combination seems well balanced to my eye.

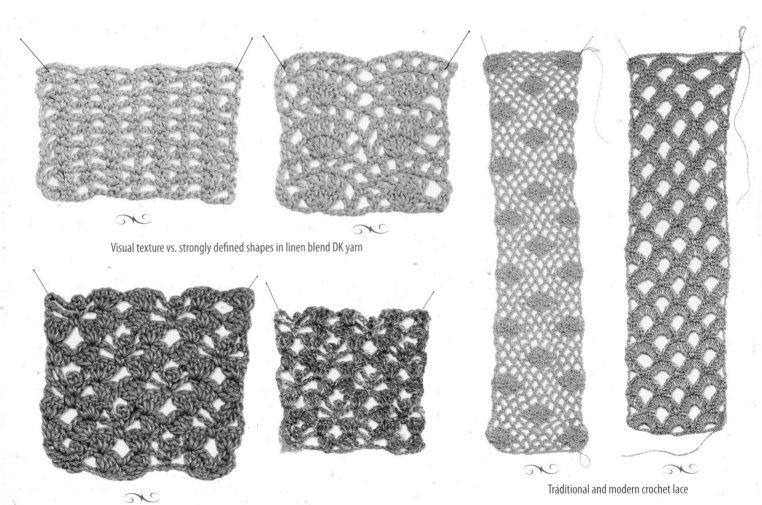

Visual texture vs. strongly defined shapes in linen blend DK yarn

Traditional lacy stitch pattern with bobbles

Traditional and modern crochet lace

45

Pattern Density

The density of a stitch pattern is a very important factor in determining how crochet fabric looks and behaves.

The linen/synthetic blend yarn on the left provides plenty of visual interest by itself, with a braided look and variation in shine between strands. It's worked up in three patterns with varying degrees of density. In the first, the fans are quite close; in the second, they are given more space; and in the third, the surrounding space is increased more and a picot is added between fans.

Each swatch has a unique appearance and each drapes differently. Picture an appropriate use for each fabric—a jacket for the densest, a scarf for the medium dense, and a shawl for the most open. I'm particularly fond of the most open swatch, where the yarn's qualities are shown off by the open stitches and picots.

Patterns in New Guises

This traditional stitch pattern—a lacy openwork shape offset by solid blocks—is very clearly defined. Compare the traditional look of plain white sport weight yarn and a modern, variegated yarn. The clarity of the pattern is still evident in the variegated swatch even though the solid blocks look dappled.

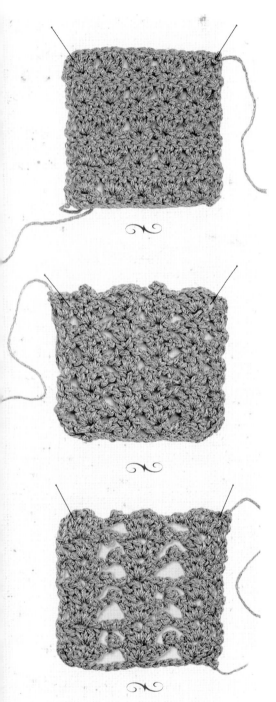

Varying degrees of stitch density

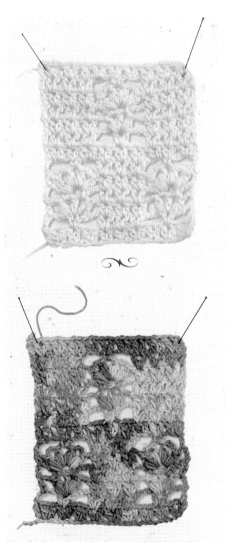

Traditional and modern use of stitch pattern

Here are some additional samples of how familiar crochet shapes are altered when seen from the perspective provided by variegated yarns.

- One swatch is a crisp cotton in a closed repeat pattern that's very simple: 1 row of dc, the next row is (sc2tog, ch 1), across. It visually defines the variegated yarn quite nicely, so we see both horizontal and vertical elements.

- The spider stitch pattern is less obvious than it would be with one-color yarn, yet I enjoy how the pattern organizes and disperses the colors of this beautifully shaded yarn.

- An open work fan pattern is used with a variegated ribbon yarn in another swatch. It may take more time for the eye to find the pattern here, yet there's interesting interplay between color and pattern in this swatch.

Simple closed pattern

Spider stitch pattern

Open work fan pattern

The next four swatches play with the elements of stitch definition, pattern clarity, pattern density, and crisp visuals as opposed to more blurred effects. The top swatches are solid colored yarns that have very strong stitch definition. Both swatches feature well-defined stitches, shapes, and movement.

- The gold, fingering weight swatch lends itself to a denser pattern without sacrificing drape.

- The lime, worsted weight swatch drapes well because the pattern is more open.

The variegated swatches were trickier. The darker one, a tightly plied worsted, has strong color and texture. It features a diagonal post stitch which imposes structure on the variegations. The lighter swatch, a yarn with variations in thickness, was crocheted with a more open stitch pattern and exhibits more subtle color changes.

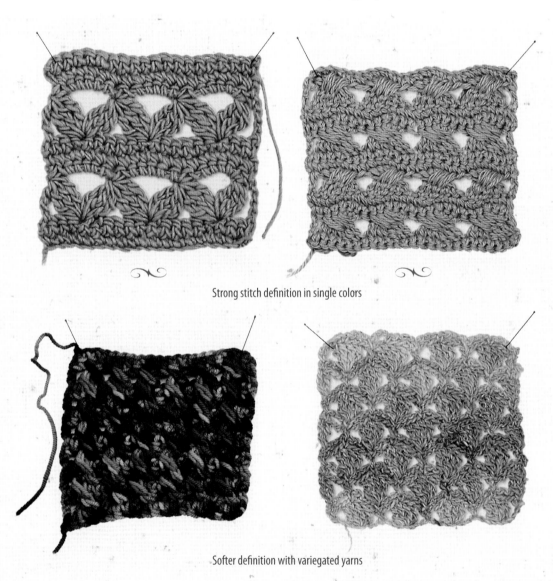

Strong stitch definition in single colors

Softer definition with variegated yarns

Color Work in Crochet

Many of the graphic elements we've discussed so far can be heightened with color changes. Almost every stitch dictionary has a special section showing stitch patterns built around color work. Even with simple rows of plain, same-height stitches, we can create visual definition simply by changing colors to make stripes in different ways.

Rows of half double crochet stitches—three rows for the wider stripe and one row for the thin stripe—are one simple variation. The backs of the half double crochet stitches add an additional visual dimension, which can be seen in every other row on the wider stripes. Further, the wider stripes are made with a multicolored yarn; without the black stripe, the fabric would look busy but bland. It's the color contrast that makes it interesting.

• Stripes can be worked on the diagonal by increasing stitches on one edge of the work and decreasing on the other.

• Do stripes have to be straight? In crochet, of course not! Using stitches of graduated heights in a random fashion across each row, we get a wavy stripe reminiscent of animal skin.

• Additional layers of geometry and visual interest can be created using the technique of mitered squares with stripes.

• Yet another interesting striping effect is to work a thinner yarn around a bulky one. The result is a woven look.

It's a short step from stripes to plaid. Plaid originally derives from the Scottish Tartan, and is a distinct weaving pattern characterized by crisscrossed stripes formed by an arrangement of the warp and weft threads. Plaids are sensational for color work, and have been created in crochet since at least the 1960s. With the greater variety of fibers available now, we can make our plaids as traditional as a Scottish kilt or as "out there" as imagination allows.

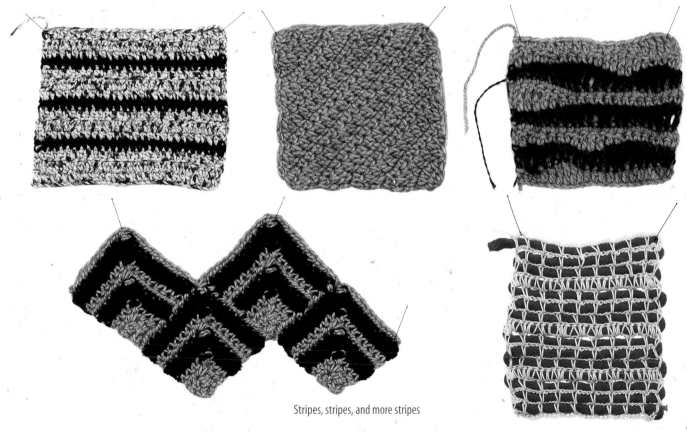

Stripes, stripes, and more stripes

To obtain a similar plaid effect in crochet, we can make an open work grid, similar to filet work, and then weave strands of yarn through it (see page 66). The lime, yellow, and white swatch shows a different approach. It uses a thinner stripe of hand-dyed variegated yarn alternating with a wider stripe of single-color mohair, all worked in single crochet. An additional stripe is then worked vertically using surface crochet in a very lightweight mohair.

Surface crochet is a method for working chains over your completed fabric. The working yarn is kept behind the fabric, then drawn up through the fabric and the loop on the hook.

Another variation—it's not strictly a plaid—uses similar crisscross stripes, where vertical stripes are created using post stitches. This adds a layer of dimension to the striping. Dimension is also present in the horizontal stripes, which are single crochet rows worked in the front and back loops.

Color Work and Spike Stitches

Stripes can be combined with other techniques to create more complex designs. Spike stitches are useful and versatile tools for color work. I've used them to mimic ethnic fabrics in the projects on page 60.

To make spikes, single crochet stitches are not worked in the preceding row as they are normally, but into stitches two, three, or even four rows below. The two "legs" of the single crochet stitch are thereby stretched over the intervening rows, adding a decorative element on the surface.

Fiddling with spike stitches I came up with these patterns, which are similar to the traditional herringbone pattern. I made several spike stitch swatches before I came up with patterns that are similar to a traditional herringbone pattern. The spike stitches are worked over a contrasting color to create a clearly visible V-shape that imitates herringbone. Horizontal stripes of plain hdc add visual interest to the fabric.

Surface crochet striping

Stripes with post stitches

Herringbone patterns using spike stitches

Tunisian Simple Stitch

A particularly interesting graphic is created with Tunisian crochet, a technique worked with a long hook that is a cross between knitting and crochet. Although there are many Tunisian stitches with different effects, I'm partial to Tunisian Simple Stitch (TSS) because of the clear geometry of horizontal rows divided by vertical strokes, called "bars" in instructions.

I work TSS with a large hook—usually no smaller than J or K, and often with even larger hooks. I find it makes lovely wearable fabric with good drape. Here are two swatches, one using ribbon yarn in TSS, the other using two very different yarns in alternating rows—a plied wool and a multistrand, multicolored novelty. Some of the interesting possibilities of Tunisian graphics with both one color and a self-striping yarn are shown in the final projects in this book (see pages 110 and 111).

Analyzing a stitch pattern for its "graphics" make us more aware of the visual elements at our disposal. Some patterns are very intricate; others have simple, clear lines of direction. Some are geometric or have other recognizable shapes. A pattern may be dense with stitches or, quite the opposite, have lots of air. Depending on the characteristics of the yarn we choose and what we want to make with it, we can use all of these visual elements to create a pleasing, functional fabric.

Adding the element of color opens up the visual potential of crochet. We can mimic and reinvent classic textile designs such as plaid or herringbone, and create stripes of all colors. The creative possibilities are limitless.

The art of crochet fabric depends on balancing the various elements at our disposal. A good starting point is to consider the degree of visual interest in the yarn. Do you want bold, simple strokes or greater detail? How does the texture or the color variation in the yarn affect the pattern? Do you want to feature the yarn more, or the stitch pattern? What kind of drape do you want? In our study of fabricology, these are basic questions we need to consider when creating crochet fabric.

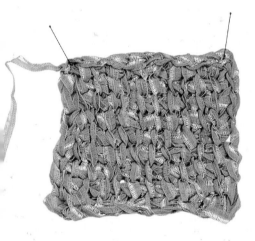

Tunisian simple stitch

tosca's lace tunic

In the Tosca's Lace Tunic, I matched a plain, light worsted weight yarn with a well-defined graphic stitch pattern: a flower surrounded by plenty of air. The strong statement is in the pattern, and the drape of the soft yarn plays a supporting role. Although the stitch pattern is bold, the color is gentle, giving the design both softness and drama. The stitch pattern also employs chain stitches, to connect one flower to the next, adding a linear element. For garments, I often prefer the flattering look of vertical lines over horizontal ones, so the garment is constructed with vertical rows.

SIZES
S (M, L) 31–36 (36–41, 41–46)"/79–91.5 (91.5–104, 104–117)cm bust

FINISHED MEASUREMENTS:
S (M, L) 37 (41¾, 46½)"/94 (106, 118)cm

MATERIALS AND TOOLS
Approx 625 (753, 879)yd/572 (689, 804)m DK weight **3** yarn in taupe,

D/3 (3.25mm) hook or size needed to obtain gauge

Safety pin

Yarn needle

GAUGE
1 patt rep = 4"/10cm; 8 rows = 4½"/11.5cm in patt

SPECIAL STITCHES
dtr2tog: Work dtr in next designated st until 2 lps remain on hook, work dtr in next designated st until 3 lps remain on hook, yo, draw yarn through all 3 lps on hook. dtr3tog: Work dtr in next designated st until 2 lps remain on hook, work dtr in next designated st until 3 lps remain on hook, work dtr in next designated st until 4 lps remain on hook, yo, draw yarn through all 4 lps on hook.

ClA: Ch 3, dtr2tog in top of last dc or Cl just made.

ClB: Dtr3tog in designated st.

What made the project particularly interesting, for me, was adding a second stitch pattern—a double crochet mesh. This impulse arose because I wanted to have shaping in the garment, but couldn't shape easily with the flower pattern. The mesh not only made shaping possible, but also echoed the lines of chains in the first pattern, while creating nice contrast and greater visual interest.

PATTERN STITCH (PATT)
Ch a multiple of 20 plus 2.

ROW 1 (WS): Sc in 2nd ch from hook, ★ch 5, sk next 3 ch, dc in next ch, ClA in dc just made, sk next 3 ch, ClB in next ch, sk next 3 ch, ClB in next ch, ClA in top of Cl just made, sk next 3 ch, dc in next ch, ch 5, sk next 3 ch, sc in next ch; rep from ★ across, turn.

ROW 2: Ch 1, sc in first sc, ★ch 5, dc in next dc, ch 3, (ClB, ch 3, ClB) in top of next Cl, ch 3, dc in next dc, ch 5, sc in next sc; rep from ★ across, turn.

ROW 3: Ch 3, sk next ch, ClB in next ch, ★ClA in Cl just made, dc in next dc, ch 5, sk next ch-3 sp, sc in next ch-3 sp, ch 5, dc in next dc, ClA in dc just made, sk next 3 ch, ClB in next ch★★, sk next (ch, sc, ch), ClB in next ch; rep from ★ across, ending last rep at ★★, sk last ch, dc in last sc, turn.

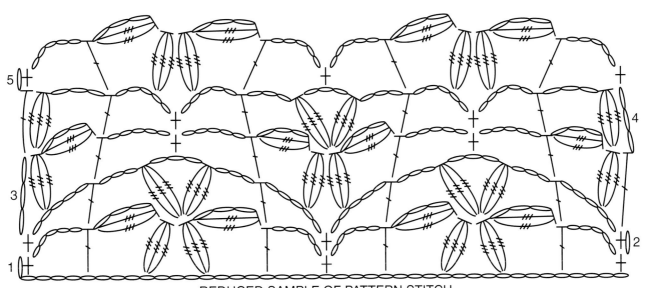

REDUCED SAMPLE OF PATTERN STITCH

ROW 4: Ch 3, ClB in top of next Cl, *ch 3, dc in next dc, ch 5, sc in next sc, ch 5, dc in next dc, ch 3, sk next ClA**, (ClB ch 3, ClB) in top of next Cl, rep from * across, ending last rep at **, ClB in next Cl, dc in top of tch, turn.

ROW 5: Ch 1, *ch 5, dc in next dc, ClA in last dc made, sk next 3 ch, ClB in next ch, sk next (ch, sc, ch), ClB in next ch, ClA in top of Cl just made, dc in next dc, ch 5, sk next ch-3 sp**, sc in next ch-3 sp; rep from * across, ending last rep at **, sc in top of tch, turn.

Rep rows 2–5 for patt.

FILET PANELS

These panels are used to create armhole and skirt shaping. The first filet row is given in detail. On subsequent filet rows in the same group, work the same height stitch into the stitch of the previous row (i.e., always work a hdc in a hdc, a dc in a dc, a tr in a tr, and a dtr in a dtr) with ch 2 between stitches. Specific instructions for how to begin and end each row are given.

SHORT ROWS (SR)

Work to the designated point, then turn as you would at the end of a normal row. When finished with the second short row, the following full row is worked into the previous short row, then work the remainder of the row into the row that precedes the short rows.

FRONT PANEL ONE

Ch 82.

Rows 1–8: Work in patt, ending with row 4 of patt—4 patt reps.

FILET PANEL ONE (FRONT ARMHOLE SHAPING)

ROW 1 (WS): Ch 7 (counts as dtr, ch 2), dtr in first dc, ch 2, dtr in next ch-3 sp, ch 2, dtr in next dc, ch 2, dtr in next ch-5 sp, ch 2, dtr in next sc, ch 2, tr in next ch-5 sp, ch 2, tr in next dc, (ch 2, tr) in each of next 3 ch-3 sps, ch 2, tr in next dc, ch 2, dc in next ch-5 sp, ch 2, dc in next sc, ch 2, dc in next ch-5 sp, ch 2, dc in next dc, (ch 2, dc) in each of next 2 ch-3 sps, ch 2, hdc in next ch-3 sp, ch 2, hdc in next dc, ch 2, hdc in next ch-5 sp, ch 2, sc in next sc, turn—21 ch-2 sps, 1 sc, 3 hdc, 6 dc, 6 tr, 6 dtr.

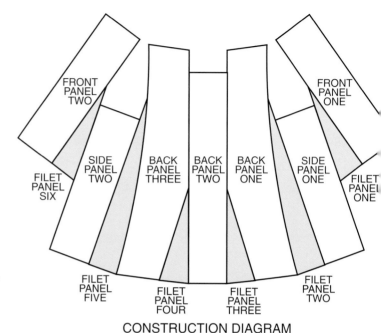

CONSTRUCTION DIAGRAM

ROW 2: Ch 2, work in Filet Pattern as established across, ending with dtr in 5th ch of tch, turn.

ROW 3: Ch 7 (counts as dtr, ch 2), work in Filet Pattern as established across, ending with sl st in last sl st, turn.

ROW 4: Rep row 2. At end of row 4, ch 39.

SIDE PANEL ONE

ROW 1 (WS): Sc in 2nd ch from hook, ch 5, *sk next 3 ch, dc in next ch, ClA in top of dc just made, sk next 3 ch, ClB in next ch, sk next 3 ch, ClB in next ch, ClA in top of Cl just made, sk next 3 ch, dc in next ch, ch 5**, sk next 3 ch, sc in next ch, rep from * to ** once, sk next (ch, dtr, 2 ch), sc in next dtr, ch 5, sk next dtr, dc in next dtr, ClA in top of dc just made, sk (2 ch, dtr), ClB in next ch, sk next (ch, dtr, ch), ClB in next ch, ClA in top of Cl just made, sk next (tr, 2 ch), dc in next tr, ch 5, sk next tr, sc in next tr, ch 5, sk next tr, dc in next tr, ClA in top of dc just made, sk next (2 ch, dc), ClB in next ch, sk next (ch, dc, ch), ClB in next ch, ClA in top of Cl just made, sk next (dc, 2 ch), dc in next dc, ch 5, sk next dc, sc in next dc, turn, leaving rem sts unworked—4 patt reps.

ROWS 2–5 (9, 13): Cont in patt. At end of last row, ch 10, turn.

FILET PANEL TWO (BACK ARMHOLE SHAPING)

ROW 1 (RS): Sc in 2nd ch from hook, ch 2, (sk next 2 ch, hdc in next ch) twice, ch 2, sk next 2 ch, hdc in next sc, ch 2, hdc in next ch-5 sp, ch 2, hdc in next dc, ch 2, hdc around ch-3 of next Cl, ch 2, hdc in top of next Cl, ch 2, hdc around ch-3 of next Cl, ch 2, hdc in next dc, ch 2, dc in next ch-5 sp, ch 2, dc in next sc, ch 2, dc in next ch-5 sp, ch 2, dc in next dc, ch 2, dc around ch-3 of next Cl, ch 2, dc in top of next Cl, ch 2, dc around ch 3 of next Cl, ch 2, dc in next dc, ch 2, dc in next ch-5 sp, ch 2, tr in next sc, ch 2, tr in next ch-5 sp, ch 2, tr in next dc, ch 2, tr around ch-3 of next Cl, ch 2, tr in top of next Cl, ch 2, tr around ch-3 of next Cl, ch 2, tr in next dc, ch 2, tr in next ch-5 sp, ch 2, tr in next sc, ch 2, dtr in next ch-5 sp, ch 2, dtr in next dc, ch-2, dtr around ch-3 of next Cl, ch 2, dtr in top of next Cl, ch 2, dtr around ch-3 of next Cl, ch 2, dtr in next dc, ch 2, dtr in next ch-5 space, ch 2, (dtr, ch 2, dtr) in last sc, turn—36 ch-2 sp; 1 sc, 9 hdc, 9 dc, 9 tr, 9 dtr.

ROW 2: Ch 7 (counts as dtr, ch 2), work in Filet Pattern as established across, ending with sl st in last sc, turn.

ROW 3: Ch 2, work in Filet Pattern as established across, ending with dtr in 5th ch of tch, turn.

ROW 4: Rep row 2, ending with sl st in last sl st. At end of row 4, ch 34 for back armhole.

BACK PANEL ONE (ACROSS SHOULDER)

ROW 1 (RS): Sc in 2nd ch from hook, ch 5, sk next 3 ch, dc in next ch, ClA in dc just made, sk next 3 ch, ClB in next ch, sk next 3 ch, ClB in next ch, ClA in top of Cl just made, sk next 3 ch, dc in next ch, ch 5, sk next 3 ch, sc in next ch, ch 5, sk next 3 ch, dc in next ch, ClA in top of dc just made, sk next 3 ch, ClB in next ch, sk next 3 ch, ClB in next ch, ClA in Cl just made, sk next ch-2 sp, dc in next hdc, ch 5, sk next hdc, sc in next hdc, ch 5, sk next hdc, dc in next hdc, ClA in dc just made, sk next (2 ch, hdc), ClB in next ch, sk next (ch, hdc, ch), ClB in next ch, ClA in Cl just made, sk next dc, dc in next dc, ch 5, sk next dc, sc in next dc, ch 5, sk next dc, dc in next dc, ClA in dc just made, sk next (2 ch, dc), ClB in next ch, sk next (ch, dc, ch), ClB in next ch, ClA in Cl just made, sk next dc, dc in next dc, ch 5, sk next dc, sc in next tr, ch 5, sk next tr, dc in next tr, ClA in dc just made, sk next (2 ch, tr), ClB in next ch, sk next (ch, tr, ch), ClB in next ch, ClA in Cl just made, sk next tr, dc in next tr, ch 5, sk next tr, sc in next tr, ch 5, sk next dtr, dc in next dtr, ClA in dc just made, sk next (2 ch, dtr), ClB in next ch, sk next (ch,

dtr, ch), ClB in next ch, ClA in Cl just made, sk next dtr, dc in next dtr, ch 5, sk next dtr, sc in next dtr, ch 5, dc in 5th ch of tch, turn—6½ patt reps.

ROW 2: Ch 8 (counts as dc, ch 5), sc in next sc, cont in patt across, turn.

ROW 3: Work in patt across, ending with 4-Cl flower, dc in 3rd ch of tch, turn.

ROW 4: Ch 6 (counts as dc, ch 3), (ClB, ch 3, ClB) in top of next Cl, ch 3, dc in next dc, cont in patt across, turn.

ROW 5: Work in patt across, ending with ch 5, dc in 3rd ch of tch, turn.

ROWS 6–9: Rep rows 2–5.

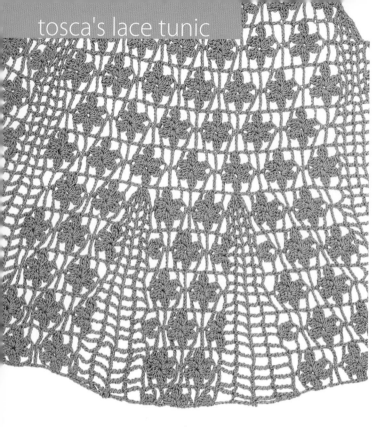

FILET PANEL THREE (SHORT ROWS)

ROW 1 (WS): Ch 7 (counts as dtr, ch 2), dtr in first dc, dtr in next ch-5 sp, ch 2, dtr in next sc, ch 2, dtr in next ch-5 sp, ch 2, dtr in next dc, ch 2, tr around ch-3 of next Cl, ch 2, tr in top of next Cl, ch 2, tr around ch-3 of next Cl, ch 2, tr in next dc, ch 2, tr in next ch-5 sp, ch 2, dc in next sc, ch 2, dc in next ch-5 sp, ch 2, dc in next dc, ch 2, dc around ch-3 of next Cl, ch 2, dc in top of next Cl, ch 2, hdc around ch-3 of next Cl, ch 2, hdc in next dc, ch 2, hdc in next ch-5 sp, ch 2, hdc in next sc, ch 2, hdc in next ch-5 sp, ch 2, sl st in next dc, turn—21 ch-2 sp; 6 dtr, 5 tr, 5 dc, 5 hdc.

ROW 2: Ch 2, work in Filet Pattern as established across, ending with dtr in 5th ch of tch, turn.

ROW 3: Ch 7, work in Filet Pattern as established across, ending sl st in last sl st, turn.

ROW 4: Rep Filet Pattern row 2.

BACK PANEL TWO (NECKLINE SHAPING)

Note: In this vertical row design, neckline shaping is achieved by making the next several rows shorter than Back Panel One at the top.

ROW 1 (WS): Ch 3 (counts as dc), ClB in first dtr, ch 3, dc in next dtr, ch 5, sk next dtr, sc in next dtr, ch 5, sk next dtr, dc in next dtr, ch 3, sk next tr, (ClB, ch 3, ClB) in next tr, ch 3, sk next tr, dc in next tr, ch 5, sk next tr, sc in next dc, ch 5, sk next dc, dc in next dc, ch 3, sk next dc, (ClB, ch 3, ClB) in next dc, ch 3, sk next hdc, dc in next hdc, ch 5, sk next hdc, sc in next hdc, ch 5, sk next hdc, dc in dc of row preceding filet panel, cont in patt over 3 more flowers, ending sc in 2nd to last sc, turn, leaving rem sts unworked—5½ patt reps.

ROW 2: Work in patt row 3 across, ending with ch 5, sc in top of tch, turn.

ROW 3: Ch 1, sc in first sc, ch 5, dc in next dc, cont in patt row 4 across, turn.

ROW 4: Work in patt row 5 across, ending with dc in top of tch, turn.

Note: This is the halfway point of garment—all shaping will be reversed when working opposite side.

ROW 5: Ch 3 (counts as dc), ClB in top of first Cl, ch 3, dc in next dc, cont in patt row 5 across, turn.

ROWS 6–8: Rep rows 2–4. Secure last lp on safety pin. Join a separate strand at beg of last row, ch 20, end off.

FILET PANEL FOUR (SHORT ROWS)

ROW 1 (WS): Picking up lp on safety pin, ch 7 (counts as dtr, ch 2), dtr in next dc, ch 2, dtr in next sc, ch 2, dtr in next ch-5 sp, ch 2, dtr in next dc, ch 2, tr around ch -3 of next Cl, ch 2, tr in top of next Cl, ch 2, tr around ch-3 of next Cl, ch 2, tr in next dc, ch 2, tr in next ch-5 sp, ch 2, dc in next sc, ch 2, dc in next ch-5 sp, dc in next dc, ch 2, dc around ch-3 of next Cl, ch 2, dc in top of next Cl, ch 2, hdc around ch-3 of next Cl, ch 2, hdc in next dc, ch 2, hdc in next ch-5 sp, ch 2, hdc in next sc, ch 2, hdc in next ch-5 sp, ch 2, sl st in next dc, turn—21 ch-2 sps; 6 dtr, 5 tr, 5 dc, 5 hdc.

ROW 2: Ch 2, work in Filet Pattern as established across, ending with dtr in 5th ch of tch, turn.

ROW 3: Ch 7, work in Filet Pattern as established across, ending sl st in last sl st, turn.

ROW 4: Rep row 2, ending with dtr2tog over last dtr and 5th ch of tch, turn—20 ch-2 sps.

BACK PANEL THREE (ACROSS SHOULDER)

ROW 1 (WS): Ch 8 (counts as dc, ch 5), sk first dtr2tog and next dtr, sc in next dtr, ch 5, sk next dtr, dc in next dtr, ch 3, sk next tr, (ClB, ch 3, ClB) in next tr, ch 3, sk next tr, dc in next tr, ch 5, sk next tr, sc in next dc, ch 5, sk next dc, dc in next dc, ch 3, sk next dc, (ClB, ch 3, ClB) in next dc, ch 3, sk next hdc, dc in next hdc, ch 5, sk next hdc, sc in next hdc, ch 5, sk next hdc, dc in dc of row preceding filet panel, cont in patt row 2 over rest of row to added ch, ending with sc in last sc; working over added ch, ch 5, sk next 5 ch, dc in next ch, ch 3, sk next 3 ch, (ClB, ch 3, ClB) in next ch, ch 3, sk next 3 ch, dc in next ch, ch 5, sk next 5 ch, sc in last ch, turn—6½ patt reps.

ROW 2: Cont with patt row 3, ending with dc in 3rd ch of tch, turn.

ROW 3: Ch 6 (counts as dc, ch 3), (ClB, ch 3, ClB) in top of next Cl, ch 3, dc in next dc, ch 5, sc in next sc, cont in patt row 4 across, turn.

ROW 4: Cont in patt row 5 across, ending with ch 5, dc in 3rd ch of tch, turn.

ROW 5: Ch 8 (counts as dc, ch 5) sc in next sc, ch 5, dc in next dc, cont in patt row 2 across, turn.

ROWS 6–9: Rep rows 2–5. At end of row 9, end off.

FILET PANEL FIVE (BACK ARMHOLE SHAPING)

Turn work. With RS facing, tie on in top of 4th Cl.

ROW 1 (RS): Ch 1, sc in same st, ch 2, hdc in next dc, ch 2, hdc in next ch–5 sp, ch 2, hdc in next sc, ch 2, hdc in next ch–5 sp, ch 2, hdc in next dc, (ch 2, hdc) in each of next 3 ch–3 sps, ch 2, hdc in next dc, ch 2, dc in next ch–5 sp, ch 2, dc in next sc, ch 2, dc in next ch–5 sp, ch 2, dc in next dc, (ch 2, dc) in each of next 3 ch–3 sps, ch 2, dc in next dc, ch 2, dc in next ch–5 sp, ch 2, tr in next sc, ch 2, tr in next ch–5 sp, ch 2, tr in next dc, (ch 2, tr) in each of next 3 ch–3 sps, ch 2, tr in next dc, ch 2, tr in next ch–5 sp, ch 2, tr in next sc, ch 2, dtr in next ch–5 sp, ch 2, dtr in next dc, (ch 2, dtr) in each of next 3 ch–3 sps, ch 2, dtr in next dc, ch–2, dtr in next ch–5 sp, ch 2, dtr in next sc, ch 2, dtr in 3rd ch of tch, turn—36 ch–2 sps; 1 sc, 9 hdc, 9 dc, 9 tr, 9 dtr. Note: This mirrors inc on opposite side.

ROW 2: Ch 7 (counts as dtr, ch 2), work in Filet Pattern as established across, ending with sl st in last sc, turn.

ROW 3: Ch 2, work in Filet Pattern as established across, ending with dtr in 5th ch of tch, turn.

ROW 4: Ch 5, dtr in next dtr, (counts as dtr2tog; dec made), work in Filet Pattern as established across, ending with sl st in last sl st, turn.

SIDE PANEL TWO

ROW 1 (RS): With RS facing, tie on in 3rd hdc from end of last row, ch 1, sc in same st, ch 5, sk next hdc, dc in next hdc, ClA in dc just made, sk next (2 ch, hdc), ClB in next ch, sk next (ch, hdc, ch), ClB in next ch, ClA in Cl just made, sk next hdc, dc in next hdc, ch 5, sk next dc, sc in

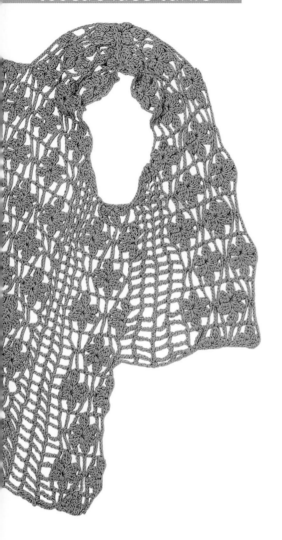

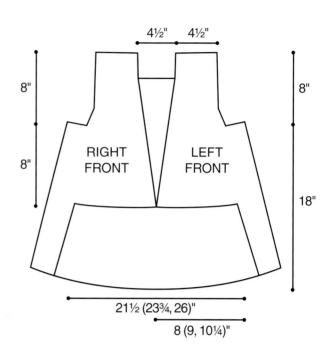

next dc, ch 5, sk next dc, dc in next dc, ClA in dc just made, sk next (2 ch, dc), ClB in next ch, sk next (ch, dc, ch), ClB in next ch, ClA in Cl just made, sk next dc, dc in next dc, ch 5, sk next dc, sc in next tr, ch 5, sk next tr, dc in next tr, ClA in dc just made, sk next (2 ch, tr), ClB in next ch, sk next (ch, tr, ch), ClB in next ch, ClA in Cl just made, sk next tr, dc in next tr, ch 5, sk next tr, sc in next tr, ch 5, sk next dtr, dc in next dtr, ClA in dc just made, sk next (2 ch, dtr), ClB in next ch, sk next (ch, dtr, ch), ClB in next ch, ClA in Cl just made, sk next dtr, dc in next dtr, ch 5, sk next dtr, sc in top of dtr2tog, turn—4 patt reps.

ROWS 2–5 (9, 13): Cont in patt. At end of last row, end off. Join a separate strand at beg of last row made, ch 12, end off.

FILET PANEL SIX (FRONT ARMHOLE SHAPING)

With WS facing, tie on in 4th ch-5 sp.

ROW 1 (WS): Ch 7 (counts as dtr, ch 2), dtr in next sc, ch 2, dtr in next ch-5 sp, ch 2, dtr in next dc, ch 2, dtr around ch-3 of next Cl, ch 2, dtr in top of next Cl, ch 2, tr around ch-3 sp of next Cl, ch 2, tr in next dc, ch 2, tr in next ch-5 sp, ch 2, tr in next sc, ch 2, tr in next ch-5 sp, ch 2, tr in next dc, ch 2, dc around ch-3 of next Cl, ch 2, dc in top of next Cl, ch 2, dc around ch-3 of next Cl, ch 2, dc in next dc, ch 2, dc in next ch-5 sp, ch 2, dc in next sc, ★ch 2, sk next 2 ch, hdc in next ch; rep from ★ twice, ch 2, sl st in last ch, turn—21 ch-2 sps; 3 hdc, 6 dc, 6, tr, 6 dtr.

ROW 2: Ch 2, work in Filet Pattern as established across, ending with dtr in 5th ch of tch, turn.

ROW 3: Ch 7, work in Filet Pattern as established across, ending with sl st in last sl st, turn.

ROW 4: Ch 1, sc in first sl st, work in Filet Pattern as established across to last 2 dtr, dtr2tog worked across last dtr and 5th ch of tch. Place last lp on safety pin. Join a separate strand in sc at beg of last row, ch 28, end off.

FRONT PANEL TWO

ROW 1 (WS): Pick up lp on safety pin, ch 1, sc in first dtr, ch 5, sk next dtr, dc in next dtr, ClA in dc just made, sk next (2 ch, dtr), ClB in next ch, sk next (ch, dtr, ch), ClB in next ch, ClA in Cl just made, sk next dtr, dc in next tr, ch 5, sk next tr, sc in next tr, ch 5, sk next tr, dc in next tr, ClA in dc just made, sk next (2 ch, dtr), ClB in next ch, sk next (ch, dc, ch), ClB in next ch, ClA in Cl just made, sk next dc, dc in next dc, ch 5, sk next dc, sc in next dc, ch 5, sk next dc, dc in next hdc, ClA in dc just made, sk next (2 ch, hdc) Cl in next ch, sk next (ch, hdc, ch), ClB in next ch, ClA in Cl just made, sk next 3 ch of added ch, dc in next ch, ch 5, sk next 3 ch, sc in next ch, ch 5, sk next 3 ch, dc in next ch, ClA in dc just made, sk next 3 ch, ClB in next ch, sk next 3 ch, ClB in next ch, ClA in Cl just made, sk next 3 ch, dc in next ch, sk next 3 ch, sc in last ch, turn—4 patt reps.

ROWS 2–8: Cont in patt. At end of last row, end off.

Weave in ends with yarn needle. Join fronts to back across shoulders with a sc seam on WS across each shoulder.

This project was crocheted with:
3 (3, 4) balls of Naturally Caron Spa (3), 75% microdenier acrylic, 25% bamboo, 3oz/85g = 251yd/230m, in Misty Taupe

aida table mats

For the Aida Table Mats, I began with a DK weight 100% cotton—a relatively thin yarn made of fiber that yields excellent stitch definition and comes in a large array of colors. Both of these factors make it great for an exploration of crochet's graphic possibilities. I also became increasingly enthralled with the design possibilities inherent in spike stitches. Spikes can be made in different lengths depending on how many rows they extend over. The simple geometry of spike stitches reminds me of ethnic prints, and I chose colors inspired by African fabrics.

The first mat alternates spiked rows with solid stripes. For the second, I found a spike stitch pattern using adjacent spikes of different lengths; they turn out looking like arrowheads. Continuing this visual element, I added another stitch pattern that forms a sharp-edged chevron shape. In sum, many visual layers are exploited in this design, a challenge I really enjoy. Surprisingly, despite the extra thickness added by the spikes, the DK weight cotton yarn turned into a fabric with great drape, and I have in mind some wearables made with these stitches. Another example of spike stitches can be found on page 103, where two hats are made with the black and white herringbone pattern on page 50.

PATTERN NOTES

For long spike stitches, it's advisable to do a practice run first to get used to regulating tension. The backs of these stitches are on the RS, so check the back of your work to see how they look. Avoid making the final top loop of the stitch too wide by bending the work when you are working the tallest of the spike stitches.

If you would like your mats to be wider, it's very simple to do so by adding more stitches in the first row and continuing to work even thereafter. Just remember to add enough stitches for a full multiple of the pattern—mat one is based on a multiple of 8, then add 7 more stitches for your foundation chain; mat two is based on a multiple of 6, then add 2 more stitches for your foundation chain. For both mats to be the same size, the number of stitches in the foundation chain should be within a stitch or two.

SKILL LEVEL
First Table Mat: Easy

Second Table Mat: Intermediate

FINISHED MEASUREMENTS
9½"/24cm wide x 15"/38cm long

TOOLS AND MATERIALS
Color A: 100yd/92m of DK weight [3] cotton yarn in yellow

Color B: 100yd/92m of DK weight [3] cotton yarn in dark brown

Color C: 100yd/92m of DK weight [3] cotton yarn in beige

Color D: 100yd/92m of DK weight [3] cotton yarn in mocha

Color E: 100yd/92m of DK weight [3] cotton yarn in copper

C/2 (2.25mm) hook for edgings

D/3 (3.25mm) hook *or size to obtain gauge*

Yarn needle

GAUGE
With larger hook, 4 sts and 5 rows of sc = 1"/2.5cm

Always take time to check your gauge.

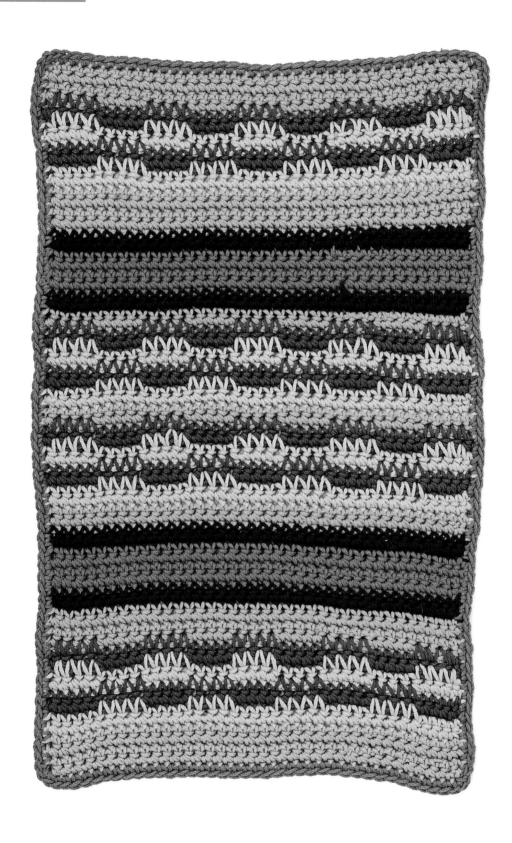

first table mat

SPECIAL STITCHES

SPIKE STITCH:

SSC2: Insert hook in corresponding st 2 rows below, pull up lp to height of current working row, complete sc as usual.

Note: On 8 rows involving two-color spikes, yarn can be carried along the side. For all other color changes, cut yarn. All rows beg with ch 1. Pattern is worked on a multiple of 8 plus 6 plus 1 ch.

With larger hook and A, ch 39 loosely.

ROW 1: Sc in 2nd ch from hook and in ea ch across, turn—38 sc.

ROWS 2-70: Work in sc and Ssc2 following chart. Tie off at end of last row.

FINISHING

At end of row 70, place lp on safety pin.

Steam block piece to make an even rectangle.

EDGING

RND 1: Change to smaller hook, take lp off of safety pin and pull through color E, ch 1, sc evenly around, working 1 sc into side of each sc stitch on the long edges, 1 sc in top of each stitch on the short edges, and 3 sc in each corner stitch, sl st in first sc to join. End off.

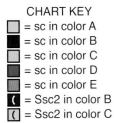

CHART KEY
- = sc in color A
- = sc in color B
- = sc in color C
- = sc in color D
- = sc in color E
- (= Ssc2 in color B
- (= Ssc2 in color C

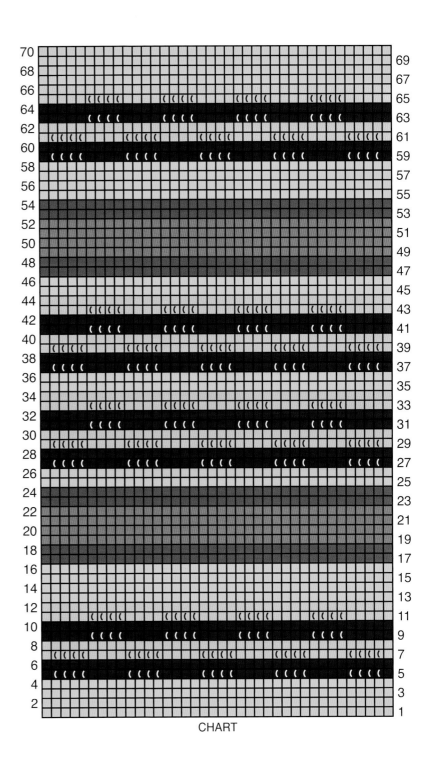

CHART

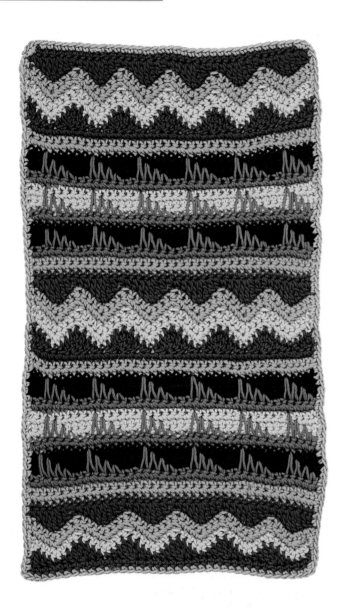

This project was crocheted with:
Tahki Stacey Charles Cotton Classic,
DK weight yarn (**3**) , 100% mercerized cotton,
1.75oz/50g = 108yd/100m

(A) 1 skein, Butterscotch (3559)

(B) 1 skein, Bittersweet Chocolate (3336)

(C) 1 skein, New Almond (3202)

(D) 1 skein, Milk Chocolate (3248)

(E) 1 skein, Tobacco Brown (3358)

second table mat

SPECIAL STITCHES

SPIKE STITCHES:

SSC2: Insert hook in corresponding st 2 rows below, pull up lp to height of current working row, complete sc as usual.

SSC3: Insert hook in corresponding st 3 rows below, pull up lp to height of current working row, complete sc as usual.

SSC4: Insert hook in corresponding st 4 rows below, pull up lp to height of current working row, complete sc as usual.

SSC5: Insert hook in corresponding st 5 rows below, pull up lp to height of current working row, complete sc as usual.

SC2TOG OVER NEXT 2 STS: Insert hook in next st, yo, draw yarn through st, insert hook in next st, yo, draw yarn through st, yo, draw yarn through 3 lps on hook.

SC2TOG WORKED ACROSS NEXT 3 STS: Insert hook in next st, yo, draw yarn through st, sk next st, insert hook in next st, yo, draw yarn through st, yo, draw yarn through 3 lps on hook.

TR2TOG: *Yo (twice), insert hook in next st, yo, draw yarn through st, (yo, draw yarn through 2 lps on hook) twice; rep from * once, yo, draw yarn through 3 lps on hook.

TR3TOG: *Yo (twice), insert hook in next st, yo, draw yarn through st, (yo, draw yarn through 2 lps on hook) twice; rep from * twice, yo, draw yarn through 4 lps on hook.

With B, ch 37 (or a multiple of 6, plus 1, plus 1 for tch).

ROW 1 (WS): Sc in 2nd ch from hook and in ea ch across, turn—37 sc.

ROW 2: Ch 1, sc in first sc, *hdc in next sc, dc in next sc, 3 tr in next sc, dc in next sc, hdc in next sc, sc in next sc, rep from * across, turn—43 sts. Change to A.

ROW 3: Ch 1, sk first sc, sc in ea of next 3 sts, 3 sc in next st, *sc in ea of next 2 sts, sc2tog worked across next 3 sts, sc in ea of next 2 sts, 3 sc in next st; rep from * across to within last 4 sts, sc in ea of next 2 sts, sc2tog over next 2 sts, turn—49 sts.

ROW 4: Rep row 3, turn. Change to C.

ROWS 5-6: Rep row 3. At end of last row, change to B.

ROW 7: Ch 4, tr in next sc (counts as tr2tog), ★dc in next sc, hdc in next sc, sc in next sc, hdc in next sc, dc in next sc★★, tr3tog worked across next 3 sts; rep from ★ across, ending last rep at ★★, tr2tog over last 2 sc, turn—37 sts.

ROW 8: Ch 1, sc in ea st across, turn—37 sts. Change to A.

ROWS 9-10: Rep row 8. At end of last row, change to D.

ROWS 11-14: Rep row 8, turn. At end of last row, change to E.

ROW 15: Ch 1, sc in first sc, ★Ssc2 in next st, Ssc3 in next st, Ssc4 in next st, Ssc5 in next st, sc in ea of next 2 sc; rep from ★ across, turn.

ROW 16: Rep row 8, turn. Change to C.

ROWS 17-20: Rep row 8, turn. Change to E.

ROWS 21-22: Rep rows 15–16.

ROWS 23-28: Rep rows 11–16, turn. At end of last row, change to A.

ROWS 29-30: Rep row 8, turn. At end of last row, change to B.

ROW 31: Rep row 8.

ROWS 32-68: Rep rows 2–31 once, then rep rows 2–8 once. End off.

FINISHING
Weave in all ends with yarn needle. There is a tendency for rows with spike sts to be slightly wider than other sections. This can be corrected by steam or wet blocking finished mat to form even-sided rectangle.

EDGING
RND 1: With RS facing, tie on A in any corner st, ch 1, sc evenly around, working 1 sc into sides of each sc stitch and 3 sc into sides of each treble stitch on the long edges, 1 sc in top of each sc on the short edges, 3 sc in each corner st, sl st in first sc to join. End off.

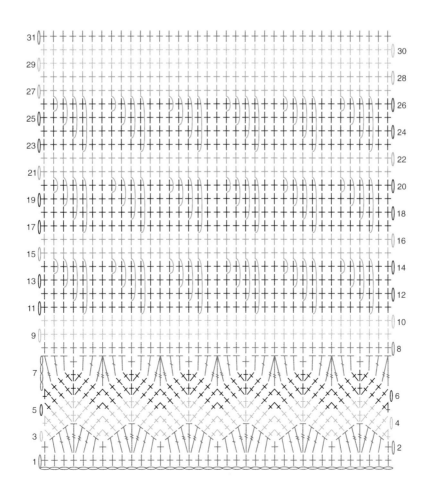

lucia scarf

There are many lovely patterns using the technique of weaving yarn through open work crochet—usually a mesh pattern—to create plaid. Crocheting the mesh is very simple—work one stitch, then one ch-1 space alternately across the row, in every row. The weaving can be done with single strands of yarn, several strands of yarn held together, or a long strand of chain stitches.

In this project I used the last strategy, because it filled up the mesh space very nicely. To get a real plaid effect, we need stripes going in both the horizontal and the vertical directions, and the stripes should be of varying widths. Where the vertical stripe meets a horizontal one of the same color, you get a solid box of that color.

This design is worked in a mohair yarn with just a bit of fuzz. The effect is soft and lacy. A fuzzier mohair would obscure the stitches more and make the scarf heavier.

SKILL LEVEL: Easy

FINISHED MEASUREMENTS
6 x 54"/15 x 137cm

MATERIALS AND TOOLS
Color A: 320yd/293m sport weight (**3**) mohair/acrylic blend in cream

Color B: 50yd/46m sport weight (**3**) mohair/acrylic blend in blood orange

Color C: 80yd/73m sport weight mohair/acrylic blend in golden

D/3 (3.25mm) hook or size to obtain gauge

Yarn needle

GAUGE
10 sts and 5 rows = 2"/5cm in Mesh Pattern

Always take time to check your gauge.

Note: The mesh is created using hdc stitches. Though it may seem counterintuitive, I found the best way to make the mesh stitches line up straight was to work hdc stitches into the ch between the stitches rather than into the top of the hdc below. Work into the ch rather than under the ch-1 space.

SCARF

With A, ch 31.

Row 1: Hdc in 5th ch from hook, ★ch 1, hdc in next ch; rep from ★ across, turn—14 ch-1 sps.

Row 2: Ch 3 (counts as hdc, ch 1), sk first hdc, hdc in next ch, ★ch 1, sk next hdc, hdc in next ch; rep from ★ across to tch, sk next ch of tch, hdc in next ch of tch, turn—14 ch-1 sps.

Rep row 2 following this color sequence: 8 more rows A, ★1 row B, 5 rows C, 1 row B, 10 rows A; rep from ★ 8 times. End off. Weave in ends with yarn needle.

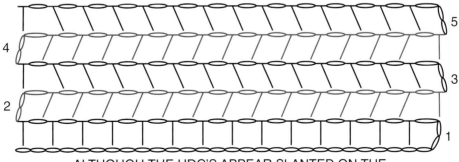

ALTHOUGH THE HDC'S APPEAR SLANTED ON THE
DIAGRAM, DUE TO THE NATURE OF CROCHET,
THEY WILL LINE UP VERTICALLY ON THE SCARF.

WEAVING

For assistance, refer to Weaving Diagram. Leaving a 6"/15cm tail, tie on A at foundation chain under first ch-1 space, then make a long chain, about 3"/8cm longer than scarf. Weave this chain through the rows of mesh, beginning by weaving over the first row and under the second row, continuing to alternate in this manner to opposite end. When done, undo any extra chains and end off, leaving a 6"/15cm tail. Pull this tail through the top of stitch on last row.

For the second woven strand, tie on in foundation ch under next ch-1 space and chain in same manner, but begin weaving under first row and over second row, continuing to end, then finish in the same manner.

Work 4 strands of A as described above, always tying on under a ch-1 space. Then tie on B at 5th ch-1 space, and weave in same manner, but do not leave a tail of 6"/15cm at either end. Use a normal tail and weave it in when done to hide this tail on both ends.

After completing one chain of B, weave a chain of C in each of the next 4 ch-1 spaces, hiding tails, and then one more chain of B. Finally, again leaving 6"/15cm tails, complete the weaving with 4 more chains of A, one in each of the rem ch-1 spaces.

FRINGE

Cut 64 lengths of A, measuring 12"/31cm. Using one strand for each fringe, fold strand in half. With WS facing, insert hook under top of last stitch and pull folded edge of fringe through to form a loop, then catch 2 strands with hook and pull through this loop to tighten. When working fringe in ch-1 space that has a tail, pull the tail through this loop along with other 2 strands, so it becomes part of fringe. Attach 32 fringes on each end, adding more fringes in center section to make up for lack of tails in fringe.

This project was crocheted with:
Lane Cervinia Softer Mohair sport weight (3) yarn, 50% mohair, 50% acrylic, 1.75oz/50g = 162yd/148m

(A) 2 skeins, Cream (3305)

(B) 1 skein, Blood Orange (3309)

(C) 1 skein, Golden (3312) <<??>>

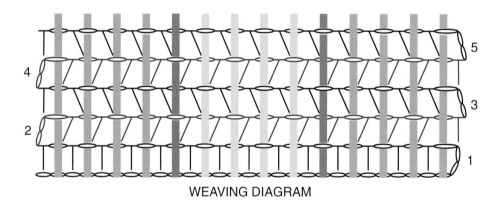

WEAVING DIAGRAM

Swatching Makes Perfect

ARE YOU FAMILIAR with this scenario? You come home from shopping at the yarn store, bags filled with several of the newest skeins that caught your eye. Some are as soft and luxurious as down, others have mouthwatering colors, or an unusual twist or texture you've never seen before. What's your next step? Whatever you do, don't relegate them to that ever-growing stash. Instead, sit down and work a swatch with your favorite size hook. Next, try a hook several sizes larger, and then go to a much smaller one. Work a few rows with a favorite stitch pattern, and finally, pull out your stitch dictionary and try some you've never done before. In short, spend some quality hands-on time with your yarn.

Believe it or not, swatching—working small trial pieces of crochet—is one of the most creative aspects of the craft. In fact, it's the only way I know of to choose the right stitch pattern and to determine the best hook size for the end product you desire. Sounds simple, right?

It is, but very few crocheters ever take the time to explore the possibilities fully, and therefore don't have the confidence to get really creative with their crochet. Those who do, have the freedom to leave patterns behind forever if they wish, invent from scratch, or adapt patterns to their own needs and tastes in yarn.

Stitch patterns for swatches marked with can be found starting on page 120.

Where to Begin?

For some, "gauge swatch" is a dreaded term that sends them off running, but let's consider why swatching is the best way to get to know a yarn. Say you have a new yarn you love, but you don't know yet what it wants to become or how it will look best. Just because it's a bulky yarn doesn't mean it will make a good jacket or scarf. The fiber content, texture, and even the construction of the yarn—whether it's tight or loosely plied or a knitted tube—can have a major influence on the end result. Before you make a decision about what to make, swatch it! If the yarn has unusual texture, or is made of a new fiber you haven't used before, these are excellent reasons to swatch. By trying different stitch patterns and hook sizes, you'll see the yarn in various guises and be able to choose the look, weight, and feel you like best. From

there, it's an easy step to deciding what kind of project it's suitable for.

Many crocheters feel swatching is a waste of time, but in my opinion it's just the opposite It's a tremendously profitable, fun, *and* study time. It's an opportunity to play with yarn and to figure out the many ways it can be worked.

I save all my swatches and hope to use most of them at some point in a design. Many crocheters think designing is beyond their abilities, and they don't give themselves permission to experiment with yarns in this way. The truth is, if you spend playful time with yarn and have a willingness to try new things, you're very likely to invent a new design. Once you have a swatch you like, turn it into something simple, such as a dishcloth or a scarf, then let your talents grow from there.

There are other reasons to swatch, of course. Have you tried substituting a yarn in a pattern other than the one originally used in the design? More likely than not, the answer is yes, and it's equally likely you had some disappointments. This is where gauge swatching is not only recommended, but an absolute must! There's simply no way to get an item to fit if you don't precede it with a gauge swatch, plain and simple. The recommended hook size is the one the designer used with *her* yarn. Because your hands and your yarn aren't the same, how can the result be?

Even if you do match the gauge of the design, but use a radically different yarn—a cotton instead of a wool, a textured yarn rather than a smooth one, or a heavily plied yarn rather than a loftier knitted tube—your

Favorite Stitch Dictionaries

Stitch dictionaries are something I can't do without. They're the record of our rich crochet heritage. No two stitch dictionaries are alike, though certain stitch patterns appear in every dictionary. And they can contain anywhere from 100 to 500 different stitch patterns. I use stitch dictionaries such as the ones pictured here from my collection when I start my swatching experiments. And you should start your own collection as well! I can't get enough of these marvelous books, and I learn something every time I see a new stitch I haven't come across before.

The Harmony Guides 300 Crochet Stitches: Volume 6, by The Harmony Guides, Anova Books, 1999

The Harmony Guides 220 More Crochet Stitches: Volume 7, by The Harmony Guides, Anova Books, 1999

The Harmony Guides Basic Crochet Stitches: 250 Stitches to Crochet by Erica Knight, Interweave Press, 2008

The Complete Book of Crochet Stitch Designs, by Linda Schapper, Lark Books, 2007

365 Crochet Stitches a Year: Perpetual Calendar, by Jean Leinhauser and Rita Weiss, Martingale, 2007

results will look very different from the original. If that gauge swatch seems like an annoyance, remember that it can save you from unpleasant and possibly costly surprises. By making a swatch with the stitch pattern used in the design, you'll see what it looks and feels like before committing to the whole project.

Whatever your starting point, your swatching experiments should begin with a few rows of simple stitches, to find a suitable hook size. We all know that even stitches are prettiest, but can you tell whether you have the best hook size? Don't rely on the yarn label, because the recommended hooks are usually determined by the knitting needle used, and will probably be too small. This goes back to the earlier discussion of the difference between knit and crochet stitches, the latter by nature being thicker, and therefore requiring a larger hook so the fabric doesn't end up stiff. You can begin by making a starting chain of approximately 20 stitches.

Make your swatch at least 6 x 6"/15 x 15cm, because it's only at that size that you can really see the characteristics of the stitch pattern, measure gauge, and get a feel for the drape of your fabric. With thicker yarns, your swatch should be larger.

Remember to count them, so you can keep your stitch count even on subsequent rows. After four or five rows, you should have a sense of whether the stitches look good. I judge the appropriateness of the hook size by how crammed or loose the stitches are. When the hook size is too small, the stitches look like sardines tightly packed in a can. If it's too big, they look scrawny. And then there's the hook where, as Goldilocks said, it's just right! The more you vary your hook choices and start to look closely at the results, the more often you'll find yourself uttering that satisfying exclamation.

If you're not delighted with how your first hook choice came out, don't rip. Just end off and start a new swatch with a smaller or larger hook. Why? It's better to start a new swatch than add on to the old one, because you won't really see the new size until after a few rows. And if you have several small swatches with different hook sizes, you can compare them and easily choose your favorite. Or you may find, as I often do, that two different sizes both have excellent uses. You might select tighter stitches for cuffs, collars, and borders, or looser ones for an edging. In any case, label your swatches with the hook size used and the source of the stitch pattern so you can easily duplicate your results later.

I'm very eager to share some tips and tricks I've discovered from my own swatching experiments. Let's begin by examining yarns more closely.

Those Tricky Yarns

Contemporary yarns come in weights from fingering to sport weight, and expand from there to DK to worsted and bulky weight. I find that many crochet stitch patterns will work beautifully in fingering or sport weight yarn, and many with a DK weight as well. Once we get into the thicker yarns, issues arise. The stitches are magnified to such a degree that they compete for attention with the stitch pattern. The scale of the pattern is blown up as well, which may or may not be pleasing to the eye. And the quest for the elusive quality of drape is more pronounced when working with heavier weight yarns. Yarns that aren't smooth— textured and novelty yarns—often defy stitch patterns too, because the stitches are poorly defined and so is the shape of the pattern. The same problems can arise with variegated yarns that make stitch patterns more difficult to discern.

Many of us want to work with these heavier gauge and novelty yarns however, so let's stop worrying about all these problems and find some crafty solutions to them.

Worsted Weight Yarns

Classic worsteds come in many styles, each with its own characteristics. Below are swatches in a soft pima cotton (at left) and a knitted-tube washable wool (at right). The cotton is worked with a G/6 (4mm) hook, the wool with an I/9 (5.5mm). The stitch pattern on top alternates singles and doubles in the same row, creating a subtle wave effect, and the bottom pattern features shells worked on the diagonal around a single crochet stitch.

- In the washable wool, the differences between the two patterns become more pronounced—there's more dimension in the shell pattern, no doubt because of the larger gauge and stiffer fiber.

- The softer cotton has more drape; the wool a somewhat stiff appearance that some people feel detracts from crochet wearables. In both fibers, the shell pattern is somewhat stiffer, because the shell stitches cause the fabric to bulk up a bit.

- Both stitch patterns work nicely in either yarn, and your choice would be determined by whether you want a plainer surface or one with more visible pattern and dimension.

If you're after wearable drape in a worsted wool or acrylic, stitches that have more air or space in them will be necessary. It's hard to get good drape with an entirely closed stitch pattern. The ripple pattern swatch below is crocheted with a size I/9 (5.5mm) hook. My choice of hook size and the amount of open space in the pattern make the swatch drape nicely.

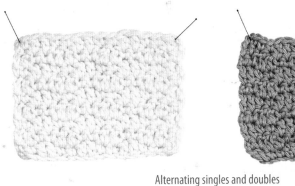

Alternating singles and doubles

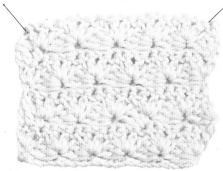

Flying shells

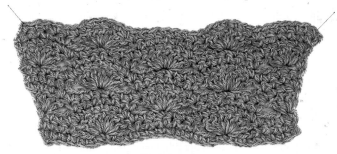

Ripple Pattern

Bulky Yarns

When we go up to heavier gauge yarns, more finesse is needed to get good results in crochet. Here are some swatches made with a "suede" yarn, a type of chenille. Its character is both rugged and cuddly. Again, we have two stitch patterns: Little Leaves and Catherine's Wheel. I worked both patterns with an I/9 (5.5mm) hook, then with a K/10½ (6.5mm). I think the smaller hook gave better results, with the larger leading to the unappetizing "worming" of chenille. I like the way both patterns look with the smaller hook, but the fabric is quite dense, workable for a bag or hat but not a wearable.

Seeking better drape, I worked another swatch, alternating rows of single and half double crochet stitches, worked into the back and front loops. It has a very nice wearable drape with an interesting surface. This was worked with an I/9 (5.5mm) hook as well, but because the stitches are shorter and involve no wrapping of yarn, there's no worming. It has the right drape for a vest or scarf.

Little leaves in suede yarn

Catherine's wheel in suede yarn

Suede yarn worked in back and front loops for drape

Of course, bulkies are not all alike. Here are samples made with a super light merino. Because it's a loosely knitted tube, its character is lofty, airy, and more suitable for wearables than plied bulkies. Two swatches are worked in Little Leaves, one with an H/8 (5mm) hook, the other with a K/10½ (6.5mm). The larger hook gives this interesting yarn the breathing room it needs. It's suitable for a scarf, but a little thick for a cardigan. Seeking more drape, I worked a swatch in big fan lace, and could definitely see this as a dramatic shawl.

Let's take on an even greater challenge—a super bulky. The swatches below consist of three chubby strands of roving plied together with added interest provided by the thick/thin weight. I used the largest hook I could find, an S (19mm), and worked seed stitch (sc, ch 1) in the back loop in each row. It had more drape than it would have with a "puny" N/13 (9mm) hook. I like the way the strands of roving show, and the visible front loops provide just enough visual structure. It could easily become a hat, jacket, or poncho. I used a P/15 (10mm) hook and double treble

stitches to see whether I could get them to drape. I alternated rows of tall stitches with rows of single crochets so that only the fronts of the tall stitches would show. All rows were worked in back and front loop alternately. There is enough visual definition despite the yarn's multiple colors. Using an even larger hook this fabric might be suitable for a jacket or a nice bag. Drape is harder to achieve when working with bulky or super bulky yarns as opposed to light weight yarns. Because of the size of the stitches, bulky yarns may not work well with various stitch patterns such as intricate lacework.

H hook

K hook

Big fan lace

Super bulky yarn with S hook

Super bulky yarn with P hook

Multistrand Yarns

Every crocheter has wondered how to handle the novelty mixes that are so intriguing but resistant to definition and drape. I experimented with a yarn made of metallic and neutral strands wrapped with a thin strand. Working with this yarn could result in a heavy, knotted-looking fabric. One swatch uses the familiar closed fans stitch pattern worked with a large hook, a K/10 1/2 (6.5mm) to create more drape. The second swatch, made with the same hook, uses the seed stitch pattern.

• In the seed stitch swatch, the squareness of the single crochet stitches imposes a pleasing regularity on this intricate yarn.

• In the closed fans pattern (at bottom) the stitches are farther apart which works well with this very complex yarn. The way the fans face multiple directions is an interesting feature.

Here's another novelty yarn made with three different fibers, not stranded together, but running alternately one after the other. One is highly textured, another is made of ribbon, and the last is plain black and white. It's worked with a K/10

1/2 (6.5mm) hook in double crochet alternating with filet double crochet. The alternation of two fabrics adds a touch of visual interest and the open work rows lend more drape. It would make a sensational scarf.

Because multistrand yarns are each so individual, it's hard to extract any rules about how to work with them. Clearly, complex stitch patterns should be avoided, and if they're heavy in weight you'll need a large hook for drape. Beyond that, it's all about experimenting with various simpler patterns, front and back loop effects, and longer versus shorter stitches, until you find a combination that looks pleasing and has the right feel for the project you have in mind.

Multistrand yarn with seed stitch

Showcasing the fabrics of a novelty yarn

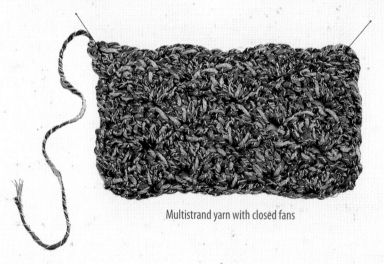

Multistrand yarn with closed fans

Tape and Ribbon Yarns

In this special category, the yarns are wide and flat, from very broad and thin to fairly narrow but thick. The main thing to keep in mind about tape yarns is that stitches look very different because the strand isn't tubular. Some stitches may not work at all with these yarns, but you can also get some interesting, novel effects with them.

Here are two swatches made with tape yarns. The red is a soy silk, rather narrow and thin; the lavender is thicker but narrower, with a bit of texture. Both swatches are worked in the same stitch patterns with the same size hook, a G/6 (4mm).

The upper section of each swatch is simple double crochet V-stitches; the bottom alternates 3-hdc fans with 3 sc. You can see both closed and open work with these tape yarns. I find the knotty texture to the stitches appealing, but I'd stay away from more complex patterns with these yarns. Drape is excellent with both of these yarns.

Ribbon yarns, a subcategory of tape yarns, resist stitch definition. Made with fine-weight fabric, they may be quite wide, and often come in lovely blended colors but seldom in solids. On the right are three swatches in the same open work stitch, a strong graphic pattern featuring a diagonal shell made around the post. I'm enthralled by the diagonal lines created with this pattern; with stitches moving in different directions in each row, the pattern definition is clearer and more visually interesting. You can see they're quite different, due mainly to the difference in width of the yarns.

The pink/blue is a delicate thin ribbon; the purple is much wider. In the purple, the stitches are more distorted, but the ribbon puffs out in a manner that I like. Just for comparison, I've included the same stitch pattern in a smooth, high-definition cotton.

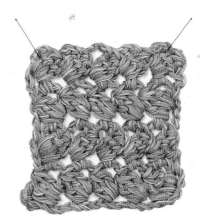

Ribbon yarns

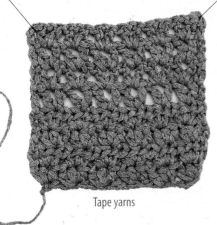

Tape yarns

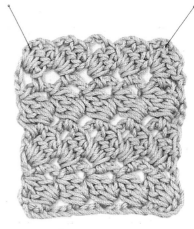

Cotton yarn

Variegated and Self-Striping Yarns

Variegated yarns have color changes at either short or longer intervals, which cause a dappled look when worked up, but they can blur the clarity of both stitches and patterns. On the other hand, it's great fun to swatch with them and see how to make the colors work in various stitch patterns.

I've worked a swatch in a multistrand yarn with plied strands of three colors and color changes every few inches. The dappled effect in the rows of plain stitches is pretty. For contrast, an angled bobble pattern at the bottom creates more dimension and heightens the color changes in the yarn. I like both sections and I'm tempted to work both together into a blazer, using the dimensional stitches for cuffs and collar.

At bottom is another variegated swatch in a cotton-blend yarn. Rows of double crochet are alternated with the pattern (sc, ch 1, dc) in the same stitch. Here the color changes every two or three stitches. I've found that patterns utilizing three stitches work well with variegated yarns.

Another example of color change is shown in this hand-painted yarn using a five-star marguerite stitch. The color changes land right on or close to each completed marguerite. How did I discover this? By swatching, of course.

Multistrand yarn with plain stitches and angled bobble pattern

Hand-painted yarn with marguerite stitch

Variegated cotton-blend yarn

Self-striping yarns have less frequent color changes than variegated yarns. By having longer spans of color, the yarn will naturally create stripes. The top swatch is made from a sock yarn, where you can see the striping effect on plain stitches—rows of doubles and half doubles alternating. In the next swatch, I used a ripple pattern to get a Missoni effect. The waves pattern looks very different with this variegated sock yarn than it would with a single color yarn.

- Fairly closed stitches are generally more successful in showing off the striping of sock yarns

- Open work lace may be hard to read, because the color changes interfere with the images made by the lace pattern.

Self-striping yarns come in all weights, so let's examine one in a wool worsted crocheted with a forked cluster pattern variation. You might think the number of stitches was carefully calculated to make most of the stripes, but they weren't. I used a random number of stitches for my starting row. The very clever strategy of self-striping yarns is to change the colors very gradually so they fool the eye into thinking there are solid stripes. You can see the subtle gradations of color at the side edges of this swatch.

Striping with plain stitches

Striping with ripple pattern

Wave pattern in variegated sock yarn

Self striping with forked cluster variation

Bouclé and Textured Yarns

Along with novelty yarns, bouclé and other textured yarns are among the most delightful looking on the ball, and most challenging on the hook. Bouclé yarns have a curly texture, created during the spinning process: several strands are plied together, but at different tensions, causing the more loosely spun strand to curl around the others.

Curls are fun, but in bouclé yarns both stitch and pattern definition are lost. Many bouclés also have a thick/thin aspect that creates further distortion of stitches. They don't work well with complex stitch patterns, which depend on regular, even-sized stitches to make the shapes clear.

Bouclés are thick by nature, so they present the same issues for drape as any bulky yarn. Even if the yarn looks relatively thin, it tends to behave more like a bulky yarn because the stitches resist lying neatly against one another.

The first question when working with this type of yarn is whether to use a hook suited to the thicker sections of the yarn or to the thinner. I tend to use a smaller hook, which leaves the bulky parts of the yarn on the backs of stitches, because they resist being pulled through. If you've ever worked with the eyelash yarns

so popular a few years ago, you probably noticed how the lashes gather at the back of stitches for just the same reason.

I crocheted a swatch made with a pastel lavender yarn that has intermittent loosely spun fibers on it. I worked alternating rows of single and double crochet stitches which resulted in two interesting and different effects on either side of the swatch. On the side where the double crochet stitches face the back, there's more fluff showing. On the side with the single crochet rows facing the back, the fluffy bits form neat, discernible lines.

If you want more fluff to show, you should work in the round; because you don't turn at the ends of rows, all the stitches face in the same direction, so all the fluff or all the smoothness can be on one side or the other as shown in the circular pink swatch. This would work very well for a hat. The fluffier part could face in, warming the head nicely, or it face out, resembling fur.

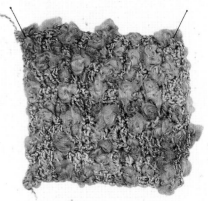

Sc stitches face the back

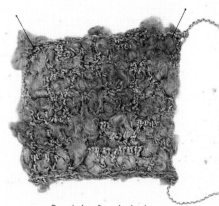

Dc stitches face the back

Bouclé derives from the French word *boucler*, which means to curl.

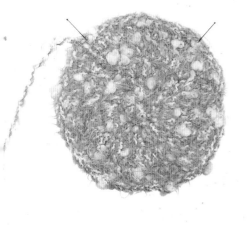

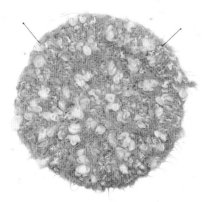

Working in the round

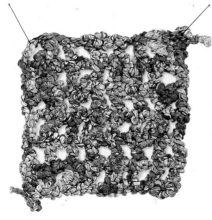

Simple filet doubles

The last swatch is also a thick/thin yarn but less fuzzy than the first sample, and heavier in weight. I pondered this yarn for a while without knowing quite what to do with it. Worked in solid stitches, it's too heavy to do much with. Following my own guidelines about swatching, I tried simple filet doubles, and I like the result. The pattern is clear and simple enough to read despite the yarn's color changes and textured surface, and has enough drape to be used for a scarf or shawl.

More complex stitch patterns aren't likely to work with most bouclé yarns. They simply have too much texture to be usable for this purpose. So what can you do?

- Control the degree of texture by changing the height of stitches.

- Experiment with your hook size to make all the texture move to one side.

- Work in the round so that all rows face the same direction, putting all the texture on the same side.

As you've seen in these swatching experiments, each yarn has a personality all its own, and to find the best use for it, swatching is the way to go. You can't judge a yarn simply by looking at a ball or skein. Swatching allows you to examine how any yarn—plain or complex—can be used to create a fabulous fabric. The clever swatcher can choose from a variety of stitches—open and closed—that interact with the yarn you've chosen to give you the finished product you desire. Creating swatches gives you a chance to experiment with stitch patterns and how they interact with variegated, novelty, bulky, or textured yarns.

You and I both know there's really no such thing as a plain crochet fabric. Even simple rows of same-height stitches have dimension and texture. Crochet stitches have a life all their own, and it's up to the us to deploy them in ways that interact most favorably with the yarn being used, and balance them with other design elements such as color, shape, dimension, and texture. It's a fantastic challenge that keeps the craft interesting and the crafter's creativity stimulated.

melisande shawl

The yarn used in this shawl is complex and textured, with varying degrees of thickness and bouclé-like nodules at regular intervals. That led me to think about large-scale, very open patterns with clear outlines, to avoid anything that might look too busy and compete with the yarn. I was intrigued by the idea of contrasting one bold pattern with another, yet retaining visual harmony. I chose two patterns that have large open areas and recognizable, simple shapes: in one, a fan; in the other, circles. The fluid drape that's ideal for a shawl was also a factor in choosing these open, airy patterns.

SKILL LEVEL: Easy

FINISHED MEASUREMENTS
Approx 15 x 60"/39cm x 152cm

MATERIALS AND TOOLS
800yd/732m worsted weight yarn in green,

C/2 (2.75mm) hook or size to obtain gauge

GAUGE
10 sts, measured from base of one fan to the next = 1½"/3.8cm; rows 1–3 in patt = 1½"/3.8cm

Always take time to check your gauge.

Note: Make the treble crochet stitches tall by drawing up first lp of stitch to ½"/1.3cm.

Note: Design is worked in two pieces, starting at center back, to be sewn together when done.

HALF SHAWL (MAKE 2)
Ch 101.

ROW 1: Ch 5 (counts as tr, ch 1), 3 tr in 6th ch from hook, ★ch 1, sk next 9 ch★★, (3 tr, ch 1, tr, ch 1, 3 tr) in next ch; rep from ★ across, ending last rep at ★★, (3 tr, ch 1, tr) in last ch, turn—9 shells; 1 half shell at ea end of row.

ROW 2: Ch 1, sc in first tr, ★ch 3, sk next st, sc in next tr; rep from ★ across, ending with last sc in 4th ch of tch, turn—50 ch-3 sps.

ROW 3: Ch 5 (counts as tr, ch 1), sk next ch-3 sp, tr in next sc, ★ch 1, skip next ch-3 sp, tr in next sc; rep from ★ across, turn—50 ch-1 sps.

ROW 4: Ch 1, sc in first tr, ★ch 1, sc in next tr, rep from ★ across, ending with last sc in 4th ch of tch, turn—50 ch-1 sps.

ROW 5: Ch 5 (counts as tr, ch 1), 3 tr in first sc, ★ch 1, sk next 4 sc★★, (3 tr, ch 1, tr, ch 1, 3 tr) in next sc; rep from ★ across, ending last rep at ★★, (3 tr, ch 1, tr) in last sc, turn—9 shells; 1 half shell at ea end of row.

ROWS 6–13: Rep rows 2–5 twice.

ROW 14: Ch 4 (counts as tr), skip next ch-1 sp, tr3tog worked over next 3 tr, ★ch 9, skip next ch-1 sp★★, tr7tog worked across next 7 tr; rep from ★ across, ending last rep at ★★, tr4tog worked over next 3 tr and 4th ch of tch, turn.

ROW 15: Ch 5 (counts as tr, ch 1), 3 tr in first st, ★ch 1, sk next ch-9 lp★★, (3 tr, ch 1, tr, ch 1, 3 tr) in next tr7tog; rep from ★ across, ending last rep at ★★, (3 tr, ch 1, tr) in top of tch, turn.

ROWS 16–17: Rep rows 14–15.

ROWS 18–57: Rep rows 2–17 twice; then rep rows 2–9 once.

ROW 58: Ch 1, sc in first tr, ★ch 1, sk next st, sc in next tr; rep from ★ across, ending with last sc in 4th ch of tch, turn—50 ch-1 sps.

ROW 59: Ch 1, sc in ea sc and in ea ch-1 sp across.

FINISHING
With WS facing, sew foundation chains of each half together.

BLOCKING
Steam block to flatten and straighten edges.

This project was crocheted with:
8 skeins of Berroco Seduce, 47% rayon, 25% linen, 17% silk, 11% nylon, 1.41oz/40g = 100 yd/91m, in Passimenterie Green (4451),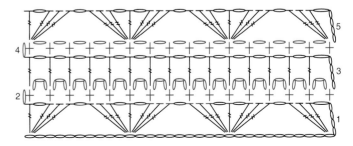

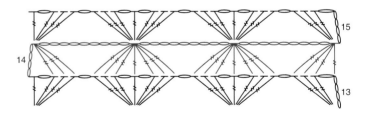

REDUCED SAMPLE OF PATTERN

chapeau lulu

In this project, I wanted to create an item with plenty of stiffness and structure rather than drape. For this reason, I chose bulky yarns, and worked with two strands at a time. Using a heavily dimensional stitch—gigantic bobbles—creates strong visual definition, despite the mix of colors; they also make the hat thick and warm. The inherent structure of crochet makes it particularly suitable for hats, as does the fact that crochet is easy to work in the round (in knitting, it requires circular needles). Unlike most crochet hats, which start at the top and increase out, this design starts at the outside and works its way in via decreases. That's because I found it much easier to work the shaping by starting at the bottom, with full-sized bobbles, then experimenting with ways to decrease them as I approached the center. This is known as "designing on the hook," a method I sometimes employ rather than working out all the details ahead of time.

This project demonstrates how to combine bulky yarns and textured stitches for a very structured, unusual-looking piece that's fun, functional, and full of character.

SKILL LEVEL: Easy

FINISHED MEASUREMENTS
Head circumference 18½"/47cm (will stretch to fit up to 22"/56cm)

MATERIALS AND TOOLS
124yd/114m of two contrasting bulky yarns,

L/11 (8mm) crochet hook or size to obtain gauge

GAUGE
3 SB + 2 hdc = 5"/13cm; 4 rows = 3"/8cm in patt

Always take time to check your gauge.

SPECIAL STITCHES
Sideways bobble (SB): (Yo, insert hook around post of st just made, draw up a loop, yo, draw through 2 loops) 5 times, yo and draw through 6 loops on hook.

Note: This stitch and the hdc stitch it is worked around count as *1 stitch* for your stitch count. In the row following the SB row, skip the bobble and work into the hdc only; don't be tempted to work into the side of the bobble or you will change the stitch count.

PATTERN NOTES
For best results when working two strands of bulky yarn, use a slippery hook; work very slowly to start to get the feel of working with thick yarn and the hook; the slower you go, the better you can get a relaxed, loose hand, which is the key to working these gigantic stitches with ease.

Hat is worked from WS.

HAT

With one strand of each yarn and smaller hook, ch 45, working tightly to measure approx 18"/46cm.

Remove hook from work. Turn the chain so that the back faces you (with the bumps on the back of the stitches showing). Shape the chain into a circle, sl st to top loop (above the bump) of beg ch. This maneuver creates a nice-looking border at the bottom of the hat and minimizes twisting of the foundation chain.

RND 1: Ch 1, as described above, work sc in top loop of each ch around, sl st in first sc to join—45 sts.

RND 2: Ch 2 (counts as hdc), hdc in next sc, SB, hdc in next sc, ★hdc in each of next 2 sc, SB, hdc in next sc; rep from ★ around, ending with hdc in last sc, sl st in top of beg ch-2 to join—15 SB.

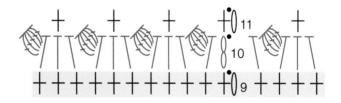

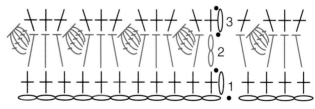

REDUCED SAMPLE OF PATTERN

RND 3: Ch 1, sc in first st, sc in next hdc, ★sk next bobble, sc in each of next 3 hdc; rep from ★ around, ending sk top of last bobble, sc in next hdc, sl st in first sc to join.

RNDS 4–7: Rep rnds 2–3.

RND 8: Rep rnd 2.

SHAPE TOP OF HAT

RND 9: Ch 1, sk first st, sc in next hdc, ★sk next (bobble and 2 hdc)★★, sc in next st (just before next bobble); rep from ★ around, ending last rep at ★★, sl st in first sc to join—15 sc.

RND 10: Ch 2 (counts as hdc), ★hdc in next sc, SB, hdc in each of next 2 sc; rep from ★ around, ending with hdc in last sc, sl st in top of beg ch-2 to join—5 SB.

RND 11: Ch 1, sc in same st, ★sk next (bobble and 2 hdc)★★, sc in next hdc; rep from ★ around, ending last rep at ★★, sl st in first sc to join—5 sc.

RND 12: Ch 2 (counts as hdc), sk next sc, hdc in next sc, SB, sk next sc, hdc in next sc, sl st in top of beg ch-2 to join. End off.

This project was crocheted with:
1 skein of Moda Dea Metro, bulky weight yarn, 94% acrylic, 6% nylon, 3.52oz/100g = approx 124yd/114m, black, (5)

1 skein of Austermann Murano, bulky weight yarn, 51% wool, 49% acrylic, 5.29oz/150g = 252yd/230m, color #10, (5)

juliette shawl

The Juliette Shawl is based on a concept perfected in Victorian times, when shawls were ubiquitous. You begin with a small triangle at the center back neck, and increase at the corners to create a triangular shawl. It's similar to working a square motif, but is worked on two sides of the square, instead of four. Three different open work stitch patterns are used to give the shawl some visual interest and drape. Puff stitches were used at the start, then puffs topped with fans, creating a pineapple shape. In Victorian shawls, there is often a large fan pattern used to form a wide edging worked on the last section of the shawl, and I followed that method here. When combining stitch patterns, it's wise to find unifying elements. These large fans form diagonal lines that are echoed in the smaller fans, so there is harmony throughout.

SKILL LEVEL: Intermediate

FINISHED MEASUREMENTS
After blocking, approx 43"/109cm across flat top edge, 20½"/52cm from point of triangle to center top

MATERIALS AND TOOLS
600yd/550m DK weight yarn, (3)

C/2 (2.75mm) hook or size needed to obtain gauge

GAUGE
Rows 1–3 unblocked = 4¼"/11cm wide, 2½"/6cm from point of triangle to flat edge

SPECIAL STITCHES
CL (tr3tog): Work 3 tr, leaving last lp of each st on hook, yo, draw through all 4 lps.

Ch 4-CL: Ch 4, tr2tog (counts as first CL of all rows in Section I of this pattern).

Open Fan (OF): In designated st, work (tr, ch 1) 3 times, tr in same st. At the beginning of a row, make OF as follows: ch 5 (counts as tr, ch 1), (tr, ch 1) 2 times, tr in same st.

Double Open Fan (DOF): In designated lp make (tr, ch 1) 7 times, tr in same lp.

PATTERN NOTES
All rows have increases at the center and sides to create a triangular shape.

Pattern begins at top neckline and is worked in three sections, each using a different pattern stitch.

SECTION I: BOBBLE-TREBLE WEB
Ch 6, join into a ring with sl st in first ch.

ROW 1: Ch 4-CL in ring, ch 4, (CL, ch 3) 2 times in ring, CL in ring, ch 4, CL in ring, turn—19 st, 5 CL.

ROW 2: Ch 4-CL in first CL, ch 3, tr in same CL, ch 5, tr in next CL, ch 5, in center CL work (tr, ch 2, tr, ch 2, tr), (ch 5, tr) in each of next 2 CL, ch 3, CL in last CL, turn.

ROW 3: Ch 4-CL in first CL, ★ch 5, CL in next tr; rep from ★ to last CL, ch 5, CL in last CL, turn—9 CL.

ROW 4: Ch 4-CL in first CL, ch 3, tr in same CL, ch 5, ★tr in next CL, ch 5; rep from ★ to center CL, (tr, ch 3, tr, ch 3, tr) in center CL, (ch 5, tr) in each CL to last CL, (tr, ch 3, CL) in last CL, turn.

ROW 5: Rep row 3—13 CL.

ROWS 6-11: Rep rows 4–5 three times—25 CL at end of last row.

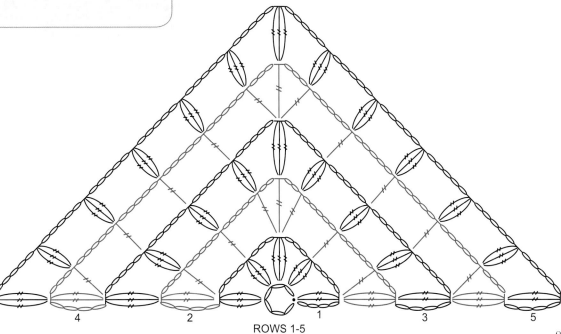

ROWS 1-5

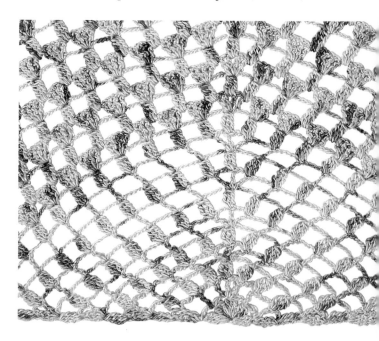

SECTION II: MINI PINEAPPLES

ROW 12: OF in first CL and in each CL across, turn—25 OF.

ROW 13: Ch 4-CL in first tr, ch 3, CL in 2nd ch-1 sp, sk (tr, ch 1 tr), ★ch 5, CL over in sp between next 2 OFs★; rep from ★ to ★ to center OF, CL in center ch-1 sp of center OF, rep from ★ to ★ to end, ch 5, CL in 2nd ch-1 sp of last OF, ch 3, CL in 4th ch of tch—29 CL.

ROWS 14-19: Rep rows 12–13 three times—41 CL at end of last row.

ROW 20: Rep row 12—41 OF.

SECTION III: FANNING OUT

ROW 21: Ch 4, ★OF in center ch-1 of next OF; rep from ★ to ★ to center OF, in center ch-1 sp of center OF work (tr, ch 1) 5 times, tr in same ch-1 sp; rep from ★ to ★ to end, tr in 4th ch of tch, turn.

ROW 22: Ch 1, sc in first tr, ★ch 2, sc in first ch-1 sp of next OF, ch 8, sk next ch-1 sp, sc in next ch-1 sp, ch 2, sc in 2nd ch-1 sp of next OF, ch 5, sk next ch-1 sp, sc in next ch-1 sp; rep from ★ to ★ to center fan, sc in first ch-1 sp of center fan, (ch 8, sk next ch-1 sp, sc in next ch-1 sp) 2 times; rep from ★ to ★ to last OF, sc in first ch-1 sp of last OF, ch 8, sk ch-1 sp, sc in next ch-1 sp, ch 2, sc in tch, turn.

ROW 23: Ch 4, ★DOF in next ch-8 lp, sc in next ch-5 lp; rep from ★ to ★ to first ch-8 lp at center, DOF in each of next 2 ch-8 lps, sc in next ch-5 lp; rep from ★ to ★ to end, tr in last sc, turn—22 DOF.

ROW 24: Ch 1, sc in first tr, ch 4, sc in 2nd ch-1 sp, ch 5, sk next 2 ch-1 sps, sc in next ch-1 sp, ★ch 8, sc in 3rd ch-1 sp of next DOF, ch 5, sk next ch-1 sp, sc in next ch-1 sp★; rep from ★ to ★ to center, ch 8, sc in sp between center pair of DOFs; rep from ★ to ★ across, ending with ch 4, sc in tch.

ROW 25: Ch 5 (counts as tr, ch1), (tr ch 1, tr, ch 1, tr) in first ch-4 lp, ★sc in next ch-5 lp, DOF in next ch-8 lp★; rep from ★ to ★ to center, DOF in each ch-8 lp at center, rep from ★ to ★ across, ending with sc in last ch-5 lp, (tr, ch 1) 3 times in last ch-4 lp, tr in last sc, turn.

ROW 26: Ch 1, sc in first sc, ch 5, sk first ch-1 sp, sc in 2nd ch-1 sp, ★ch 8, sc in 3rd ch-1 sp of next DOF, ch 5, sk next ch-1 sp, sc in next ch-1 sp★; rep from ★ to ★ to center, ch 8, sc in sp between center pair of DOF; rep from ★ to ★ across, ending with ch 8, sc in 2nd ch-1 sp of last OF, ch 5, sc in 4th ch of tch, turn.

ROW 27: Ch 5 (counts as tr, ch 1) (tr, ch 1, tr) in first sc, sc in first ch-5 lp, ★DOF in next ch-8 lp, sc in next ch-5 lp★; rep from ★ to ★ to center, DOF in each ch-8 lp at center, sc in next ch-5 lp, rep from ★ to ★ across, ending with (tr, ch 1, tr, ch 1, tr) in last sc, turn.

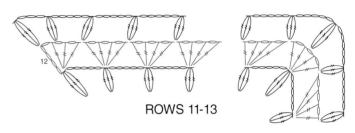

ROWS 11-13

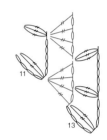

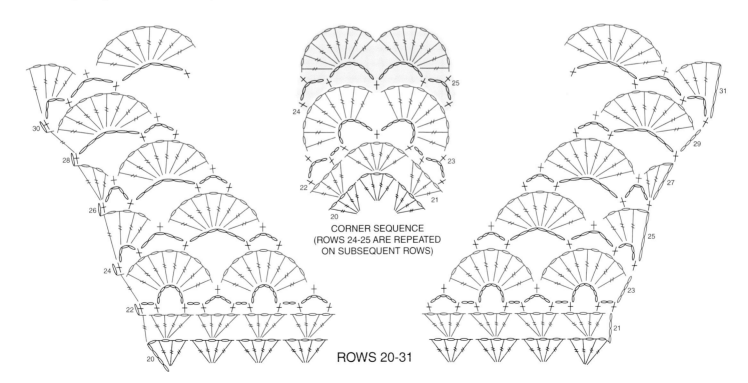

CORNER SEQUENCE
(ROWS 24-25 ARE REPEATED
ON SUBSEQUENT ROWS)

ROWS 20-31

ROW 28: Ch 1, sc in first tr, ★ch 8, sc in 3rd ch-1 sp of next DOF, ch 5, sk next ch-1 sp, sc in next ch-1 sp; rep from ★ to ★ to center, ch 8, sc in sp between center pair of DOFs; rep from ★ to ★ across, ending with ch 8, sc in 4th ch of tch, turn.

ROW 29: Ch 4, ★DOF in next ch-8 lp, sc in next ch-5 lp; rep from ★ to ★ to center, DOF in each ch-8 lp at center, sc in next ch-5 lp; rep from ★ to ★ across, ending with DOF in last ch-8 lp, tr in last sc, turn— 26 OF.

ROW 30: Rep row 24.

ROW 31: Rep row 25. End off.

Note: The size of the shawl is suitable to a small or medium. For larger sizes, rep from row 26 to desired size, ending with an odd-numbered row. Keep in mind that shawl will gain 2–4"/5–10cm in width and length with blocking.

FINISHING

Gently steam from both sides to flatten to finished measurements.

This project was crocheted with:
5 skeins of Colinette Tao, DK weight (3), hand-dyed 100% silk, 1.75 oz/50g = 128yd/117m, in marble (88)

Putting It All Together

MY STUDY OF CROCHET fabricology is ongoing. Every time I create a new design, I learn something
more about my essential tools—
yarns, hooks, and stitch patterns.
With the endless variety of stitch patterns and techniques and the steady
stream of new yarns, discoveries
never cease with crochet, and that's
why I love it.

One way to continue your education
is to study how different yarns work
with a particular design. On ravelry.
com, for example, you'll see popular
patterns made by several dozen people, each with different yarn. Ever
wonder why some work better than
others? Sometimes there's a great
match between the stitch pattern in
the design and the yarn chosen, and
at other times the combination is less
harmonious. Some patterns works
well with many different yarns, while
others seem to work only with the
yarn they were designed in, or something very close to it. Many designs
can successfully be given alternative
looks with different yarns.

In this last chapter, I conducted a
sort of design experiment, working
three designs two times in very different yarns. It allows us to see how
my "theories" come to bear on the
design process. In each case, I discuss
which elements of the design were
affected, enhanced, muted, and so on.

Stitch patterns for swatches marked with
✧
can be found starting on page 120.

Notice that I adjusted the gauge to
accommodate the change in yarns
and therefore the row and stitch
counts. Why? Even if two yarns are
called worsteds, the fibers they're
made with, and the spin, plies, and
textures, have an effect on how large
a hook you choose and the gauge you
work in. When a design is planned,
all of the details are built around the
yarn's characteristics, and the designer picks the gauge that makes that
particular yarn look best and yields
the right drape. The gauge, in turn,
determines the number of stitches
and rows needed to obtain the necessary dimensions. If a different yarn is
used, it's likely that the perfect gauge
for that yarn may be different as well.

When people substitute a yarn in
a pattern, they often try to match
gauge without giving sufficient
consideration to other characteristics
of the yarn. A general rule of thumb
is to stay close to the fiber content
and structure of the yarn used in
a design.

- If the original design is a wool or
  wool blend, don't substitute a cotton or silk.

- Don't choose a textured or fuzzy
  yarn when stitch definition is an
  important design element.

- If the stitch pattern used is an
  intricate one, make sure the yarn

you choose will provide sufficiently
clean lines to make the pattern clear.

- Most important, remember what
  you've learned: swatch, swatch,
  swatch when you first encounter a
  yarn. That will allow you to see
  how a particular yarn works with a
  variety of stitches, hook sizes, and
  patterns, and you'll be able to tell a
  lot more about whether it can work
  as a substitute for another yarn.

Not every yarn works for every
design; use the information in this
book to help you make better judg-
ments about what will work and
what won't. On the other hand, designs can be adapted to suit different
yarns, as the projects in this chapter
show, but they'll usually require
some adjustment to the pattern. If the
yarn you want to substitute works
better in a different gauge, use that
gauge and make adjustments to the
number of rows and stitches. This
skill takes time to learn and develop,
but it's well worth it.

Keep in mind that the dimensions
you're aiming for can usually vary
up to 1 inch (2.5 cm) for areas like
bust and shoulders, but less so for
close-fitting areas like neck and wrist.

As I worked on these designs with
the two yarns selected for them
in this chapter, I thought about
the issues we've looked at in previous chapters.

- Whether stitches looked attractive

- Whether stitch definition was an important element in the design

- Stitch pattern legibility

- Whether the yarn's texture would enhance or interfere with the design

- The degree to which changes in gauge would occur, and how that in turn would affect shaping and other design details

- How drape would be affected

Play with Your Yarns

If this book has inspired you to increase your fabricology skills, here is one exercise for you to try to become more adept at working with a variety of yarns: choose five appealing yarns that look really different from each other, and buy one ball of each. (Call this an educational expense.)

Open your stitch dictionaries and choose a few different stitches—a simple closed stitch, another more complex closed stitch such as ripples or waves, a simple filet stitch, and a more complicated lace.

Swatch each stitch in each yarn. Use a variety of hook sizes with each yarn. Now analyze your swatches based on what you've learned. See whether it helps you understand why some swatches look better than oth-

ers. Once you've gotten to that point, you're ready to design projects with that yarn.

- Crochet a scarf. Design and make a few scarves! They never go out of style, are simple to make, and make great gifts. From there, it's easy to graduate from a scarf to a simple vest made of rectangles.

- Design a shawl using more than one stitch pattern. Find elements that carry over from one stitch pattern to the next, and choose patterns that create visual harmony and interest, all while keeping drape in mind, too.

- Make hats. Once you understand the principle of increasing from the center out—it's a simple formula— you can use plain stitches and make a hat out of any yarn at all. Gauge and drape will be the most important considerations. Make a hat or two with plain stitches, and then make some more adding stripes.

- Bags can start off as a simple rectangle; don't concern yourself with shaping. Instead, pay more attention to the visual surface of the fabric. Challenge yourself by using more than one dimensional stitch— say, spikes and posts, or bobbles and posts. Try adding some color variation. Then find the perfect complementary strap.

- Take a pattern you already love—a lacy shawl or a sweater—and redo it in a different yarn. Consider all the elements covered and swatch the yarn to see whether it will really work. If it needs a different gauge, rework the math. Those brain cells can always use exercise!

There's really nothing to fear in crochet, as long as you don't feel that every experiment has to end in success. The whole point of experimentation is to take chances and keep an open mind about the result. You'll learn as much from things that don't work as from those that do, especially if you know how to analyze the results. My aim has been to suggest broad guidelines as well as concrete things to compare, to help you make choices and analyze outcomes. Most of all, I hope this book will give you the tools to be more comfortable building your crochet skills and realizing your crochet fantasies.

The first project is a little shrug that's simple and fun to make (it shouldn't take more than a few hours). One version, Carmen, is made from a smooth, slinky, DK weight yarn, and the other, Micaela, is done in worsted weight cotton. The stitches are super simple: rows of treble stitches alternating with single crochet post stitches worked in a special way to create subtle textural definition. I used the same stitch for the Rusalka Wrap (page 35), for the same reason.

To enhance drape, long stitches are used. Why not make it all in trebles? I'm not fond of the backs of those long stitches. By alternating with single crochet rows, all the treble stitches face forward.

The simplicity of this design makes it very easy to substitute yarns: the stitches don't need to be super defined, and there's no complex pattern to make legible. Perhaps the only thing to consider would be sufficient stitch definition to help the single crochet post rows show up. The tall stitches will give drape to any yarn, though I'd hesitate to go up to a bulky weight. Depending on the weight and fiber, you'd have to adjust the gauge for maximum attractiveness of stitches and change the stitch and row counts accordingly.

Naturally, the two versions differ, but both make a useful wearable. The crimson color and slinky feel of the lighter weight yarn gives Carmen a dressier, sexier look. Micaela, made in cotton yarn, is more casual. It's also made of hardier fabric and probably will last longer than its showy counterpart. Both versions drape nicely because of the long stitches, and the single crochet rows add sufficient definition in both cases. It's especially needed in Micaela, where the tweedy color effect can cause an indistinct visual surface.

carmen

The shrug is made in one piece in vertical rows, each row going from the bottom front, up and over the shoulder to the bottom back. Narrower shaping for the torso is achieved with shorter stitches worked at both ends of rows. Increases are made at the center of alternate rows for shoulder slope shaping. At the neckline, there's a divide when the center back is worked separately; then after the neck opening, the front is added back to work the second shoulder.

SKILL LEVEL: Easy

SIZES
S (M, L, XL)

FINISHED MEASUREMENTS:
Bust 34 (40, 48, 54)"/87 (104, 122, 137)cm

Length 13"/33cm

MATERIALS AND TOOLS
Approx 600 (755, 910, 1040)yd/549 (691, 832, 951)m DK weight yarn in red, (3)

D/3 (3.25mm) hook or size to obtain gauge

Stitch markers

Sewing needle and matching sewing thread

2 buttons approx 1"/3cm in diameter

GAUGE
20 sts = 4"/10cm; 6 rows in patt at the middle of the rows = 2½"/7cm

Always take time to check your gauge.

SPECIAL STITCHES
Special front post sc (SFPsc): Insert hook from back to front in first tr, complete sc (first SFPsc made); *insert hook from front to back in same tr, then insert hook from back to front in next tr, complete sc (SFPsc made); rep from * for each additional SFPsc.

Extended dc (Exdc): Yo, insert hook in next st and draw lp through, yo and draw through 1 lp, (yo and draw though 2 lps) twice.

carmen

FIRST SIDE

Ch 133.

ROW 1 (RS): Tr in 5th ch from hook and in ea ch across, turn—130 sts.

ROW 2: Ch 1, SFPsc in ea st across, turn—130 SFPsc.

Count 65 st to find exact center and place marker between the 65th and 66th st. After completing ea row, move marker up to next row and keep at center.

ROW 3: Ch 3, dc in ea of next 11 sc, Exdc in ea of next 2 sc, tr in ea sc across to st before marker, 2 tr in ea of next 2 sc, tr in ea sc to last 14 sts, Exdc in ea of next 2 sc, dc in ea sc to end, ch 1, turn—132 sts.

ROW 4: Rep row 2, turn.

ROW 5: Ch 3, dc in ea of next 7 sc, Exdc in ea of next 2 sc, tr in ea sc across to st before marker, 2 tr in ea of next 2 sc, tr in ea sc to last 10 st, Exdc in ea of next 2 sc, dc in ea sc to end, ch 1, turn—134 sts.

ROWS 6–13 (6–17, 6–21, 6–25): Rep rows 2–5 (2 [3, 4, 5] times)—142 (146, 150, 154) sts at end of last row.

ROW 14 (18, 22, 26): Rep row 2.

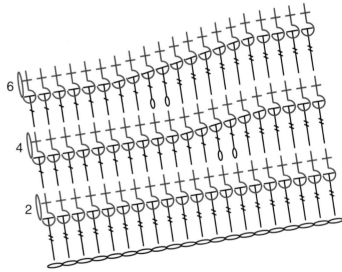

CENTER BACK

ROW 1: Ch 3, dc in ea of next 11 sc, Exdc in ea of next 2 sc, tr in ea sc to marker, turn, leaving rem sts unworked—71 (73, 75, 77) sts.

ROW 2: Ch 1, rep row 2.

ROW 3: Ch 3, dc in ea of next 8 sc, Exdc in ea of next 2 sc, tr in ea sc across, turn.

ROW 4: Ch 1, rep row 2.

ROWS 5–12: Rep rows 1–4 twice.

SECOND SIDE

ROW 1: Rep row 1 of Center Back, place last lp on safety pin. Tie on a separate strand of yarn around the post of last tr made, ch 71 (73, 75, 77). End off.

CONT ROW 1: Pick up lp on safety pin, sc in ea ch across, turn—142 (146, 150, 154) sts.

ROW 2: Ch 1, FPsc in ea st to end—142 (146, 150, 154) sts. Place marker at center between 71st and 72nd sts (73rd and 74th sts, 75th and 76th sts, 77th and 78th sts).

ROW 3: Ch 3, dc in ea of next 7 sc, Exdc in ea of next 2 sc, tr in ea sc across to 2 sts before marker, (tr2tog in next 2 sts) twice, tr in ea sc to last 10 sts, Exdc in ea of next 2 sc, dc in ea st to end, turn—140 (144, 148, 152) sts.

ROW 4: Rep row 2, moving marker to center of row.

ROW 5: Ch 3, dc in ea of next 11 sts, tr in ea sc across to 2 sts before marker (tr2tog in next 2 sts) twice, tr in ea sc to last 14 sts, Exdc in ea of next 2 sc, dc in ea sc to end, turn—138 (142, 146, 150) sts.

ROW 6: Rep row 2, moving marker to center of row.

ROWS 7–14 (7–18, 7–22, 7–26): Rep Second Side rows 3–6 (2 [3, 4, 5] times)—130 sts at end of last row.

ROW 15 (19, 23, 27): Ch 4, tr in ea st across—130 tr. End off.

FINISHING

Fold fronts down at shoulders. Place markers 7 (7½, 8, 8½)"/18 (19, 21, 22)cm below shoulder on ea side of front and back. Sew side seams from bottom edge up to markers on each side.

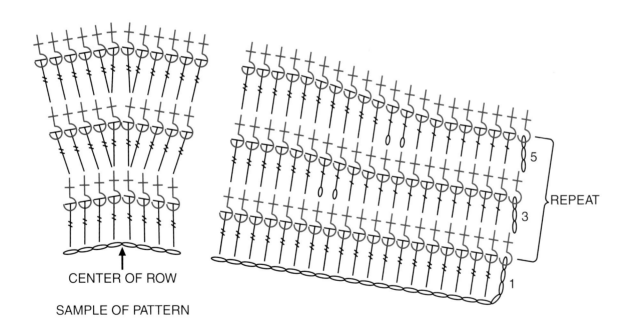

CENTER OF ROW

SAMPLE OF PATTERN

REPEAT

5

3

1

BELT

On right front of garment locate the tops of sts in row 3. To begin the small belted piece of this design, work into the tops of these sts. Hold the work so the bottom is to your right (opposite if you're left-handed) and tie on in first st of this row.

ROW 1: Ch 4 (counts as tr), skip first st, tr in ea of next 5 sts, turn—6 tr.

ROW 2: Ch 1, SFPsc in ea tr across, sc in top of tch, turn—6 sts.

ROWS 3-8: Rep rows 1–2 (3 times). End off.

Note: Feel free to make belt longer for a looser fit.

Sew one button over attached end of belt as shown. Sew opposite button directly onto body of shrug at bottom left corner. Use space between 3rd and 4th tr sts on unattached end of belt for buttonhole.

This project was crocheted with:
3 (4, 4, 5) skeins Aslan Trends Class DK weight yarn, 55% cotton, 45% viscose, 3½oz/100g = 240yd/220m, in Tomato (8), (**3**)

micaela

SIZES: S (M, L, XL)

FINISHED MEASUREMENTS:
Bust 34 (38, 42, 46)"/87 (97, 107, 117)cm

Length 13½"/35cm

MATERIALS AND TOOLS
Approx 400 (450, 500, 550)yd/366 (412, 458, 503)m worsted weight cotton yarn in blue/white, (4)

F/5 (3.75mm) crochet hook or size to obtain gauge

Stitch markers

Sewing needle and matching sewing thread

2 buttons approx 1"/3cm in diameter

GAUGE
16 sts = 4"/10cm; 8 rows = 4"/10cm

Always take time to check your gauge.

SPECIAL STITCHES
Special front post sc (SFPsc): Insert hook from back to front in first tr, complete sc (first SFPsc made); *insert hook from front to back in same tr, then insert hook from back to front in next tr, complete sc (SFPsc made); rep from * for each additional SFPsc.

Extended dc (Exdc): Yo, insert hook in next st and draw lp through, yo and draw through 1 lp, (yo and draw though 2 lps) twice.

FIRST SIDE
Ch 113.

ROW 1 (RS): Tr in 5th ch from hook and in ea ch across, turn—110 sts.

ROW 2: Ch 1, SFPsc in ea st across, turn—110 SFPsc.

Count 55 sts to find exact center and place marker between the 55th and 56th st. After completing ea row, move marker up to next row and keep at center.

ROW 3: Ch 3, dc in ea of next 8 sc, Exdc in ea of next 2 sc, tr in ea sc across to st before marker, 2 tr in ea of next 2 sc, tr in ea sc to last 11 sts, Exdc in ea of next 2 sc, dc in ea sc to end, ch 1, turn—112 sts.

ROW 4: Rep row 2, turn.

ROW 5: Ch 3, dc in ea of next 4 sc, Exdc in ea of next 2 sc, tr in ea sc across to st before marker, 2 tr in ea of next 2 sc, tr in ea sc to last 9 st, Exdc in ea of next 2 sc, dc in ea sc to end, ch 1, turn—114 sts.

ROWS 6–11 (6–13, 6–15, 6–17): Rep rows 2–5 (1 [1, 2, 2] times); then rep rows 2–3 (0 [1, 0, 1] times)—120 (122, 124, 126) sts at end of last row.

ROW 12 (14, 16, 18): Rep row 2.

CENTER BACK
Row 1: Ch 3, dc in ea of next 8 sc, Exdc in ea of next 2 sc, tr in ea sc to marker, turn, leaving rem sts unworked—60 (61, 62, 63) sts.

ROW 2: Ch 1, rep row 2.

ROW 3: Ch 3, dc in ea of next 4 sc, Exdc in ea of next 2 sc, tr in ea sc across, turn.

ROW 4: Ch 1, rep row 2.

ROWS 5–8: Rep rows 1–4.

ROW 9: Rep row 1.

SECOND SIDE

ROW 1: Rep row 3 of Center Back, place last lp on safety pin. Tie on a separate strand of yarn around the post of last tr made, ch 60 (61, 62, 63). End off.

CONT ROW 1: Pick up lp on safety pin, sc in ea ch across, turn—120 (122, 124, 126) sts.

ROW 2: Ch 1, FPsc in ea st to end—120 (122, 124, 126) sts. Place marker at center between 60th and 61st (61st and 62nd, 62nd and 63rd, 63rd and 64th) sts.

ROW 3: Ch 3, dc in ea of next 4 sc, Exdc in ea of next 2 sc, tr in ea sc across to 2 sts before marker, (tr2tog in next 2 sts) twice, tr in ea sc to last 7 sts, Exdc in ea of next 2 sc, dc in ea st to end, turn—118 (120, 122, 124) sts.

ROW 4: Rep row 2, moving marker to center of row.

Row 5: Ch 3, dc in ea of next 8 sts, tr in ea sc across to 2 sts before marker (tr2tog in next 2 sts) twice, tr in ea sc to last 11 sts, Exdc in ea of next 2 sc, dc in ea sc to end, turn—116 (118, 120, 122) sts.

ROW 6: Rep row 2, moving marker to center of row.

ROWS 7–12 (7–14, 7–16, 7–18): Rep Second Side rows 3–6 (1 [2, 2, 3] times); then rep rows 3–4 (1 [0, 1, 0] times)—110 sts at end of last row.

ROW 13 (15, 17, 19): Ch 4, tr in ea st across—110 tr. End off.

FINISHING

Fold fronts down at shoulders. Place markers 7 (7½, 8, 8½)"/18 (19, 21, 22)cm below shoulder on ea side of front and back. Sew side seams from bottom edge up to markers on each side.

BELT

On right front of garment locate the tops of sts in row 3. To begin the small belted piece of this design, work into the tops of these sts. Hold the work so its bottom is to your right (opposite if you're left-handed) and tie on in first st of this row.

ROW 1: Ch 4 (counts as tr), skip first st, tr in ea of next 5 sts, turn—5 tr.

ROW 2: Ch 1, SFPsc in ea tr across, sc in top of tch, turn—5 sts.

ROWS 3–6: Rep rows 1–2 twice. End off.

Note: Feel free to make this belt longer to alter fit. Sew one button over attached end of belt as shown. Sew opposite button directly onto body of shrug at bottom left corner. Use space between 3rd and 4th tr sts on unattached end of belt for buttonhole.

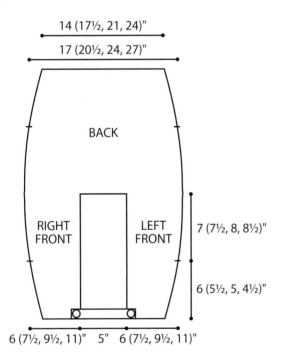

14 (17½, 21, 24)"

17 (20½, 24, 27)"

BACK

RIGHT FRONT   LEFT FRONT

7 (7½, 8, 8½)"

6 (5½, 5, 4½)"

6 (7½, 9½, 11)"   5"   6 (7½, 9½, 11)"

This project was crocheted with:
6 (6, 7, 7) balls Rowan Yarn's Cotton Jeans, 100% cotton (**4**), 1¾oz/50g = 82yd/72m, in Shingle (368)

Two hats were inspired by my experimentations with spike stitches. I spent several days working on swatches until I had one I really liked. I noticed that with the normal method of working spike stitches, they didn't align, but were off-set slightly. To counter this, I worked them directly into the center of the spike below, resulting in a strong line of color. I interrupted these spiked rows with a row of taller stitches—half doubles—in the second color, creating a counterbalancing stripe.

Stitch definition and pattern clarity are important in this pattern, so I used smooth yarns. To keep the herringbone pattern throughout, the top of the hat is created in an unconventional manner: instead of being worked in the round, it's worked in rows.

103

For Faust I chose worsted black and off-white wool blends to create a unisex look with an ethnic design. Marguerite is made with a wool blend that's a little thinner (though still considered worsted) and has a bit of shine and stretch to it. The slight difference in yarn weight meant that the gauge was different in the two versions, and some adjustments had to be made to get the proper dimensions for fit.

Even so, Faust is larger and meant for a male head, while Marguerite is smaller, though it will fit a head larger than its dimension because the yarn is stretchy. In Marguerite I thought it would be nice to feature both the front and the back of the pattern, so I added extra rows for a rolled-up brim.

faust

SKILL LEVEL: Easy

FINISHED MEASUREMENTS
Head circumference 22"/56cm

MATERIALS AND TOOLS
Color A: 196yd/180m worsted weight cotton yarn in black, (4)

Color B: 196yd/180m worsted weight cotton yarn in cream, (4)

H/8 (5mm) crochet hook or size to obtain gauge

GAUGE
11 sts in patt = 4"/10cm; 5 rows in patt = 1¼"/3cm

Always take time to check your gauge.

SPECIAL STITCHES
Ssc2: Insert hook in corresponding st 2 rows below, pull up lp to height of current working row, complete sc as usual.

FLhdc2tog: (Yo, insert hook in front lp of next st, draw up lp, yo, draw through 2 lps) twice (3 lps on hook), yo, draw through all 3 lps on hook.

Note: Change color and cut yarn at the end of every row. Refrain from weaving in ends as you go, which may distort spike stitches. Instead, weave them in at the end.

CROWN

Note: On all rows with color A (odd-numbered rows in increase section), first and last spike sts are worked as Ssc2 in top of sc 2 rows below, others are worked into the "V" of prev spike 2 rows below. When working these stitches, the V to be worked into is slightly to the left.

With A, ch 8.

ROW 1: Sc in 2nd ch from hook and in ea ch across—7 sc. Drop A, join B.

ROW 2: With B, ch 1, 2 sc in first sc, sc in ea sc across, 2 sc in last sc—9 sc. Drop B, join A.

ROW 3: With A, ch 1, 2 sc in first sc, sc in next sc, ★Ssc2 in next st, sc in next sc; rep from ★ across, ending with 2 sc in last sc—11 sts. Drop A, join B.

ROW 4: With B, ch 1, 2 sc in first sc, sc in next sc, ★Ssc2 in next sc, sc in next sc; rep from ★ across, ending with 2 sc in last sc, turn—13 sts. Drop B, join A.

ROW 5: Rep row 3—15 sts. Drop A, join B.

ROW 6: With B, ch 2 (counts as hdc), FLhdc in first sc, FLhdc in ea sc across, ending with 2 FLhdc in last sc, turn—17 hdc. Drop B, join A.

ROW 7: With A, ch 1, 2 sc in first hdc, sc in ea hdc across, ending with 2 sc in top of tch—19 sc. Drop A, join B.

ROW 8: With B, ch 1, sc in ea sc across, turn. Drop B, join A.

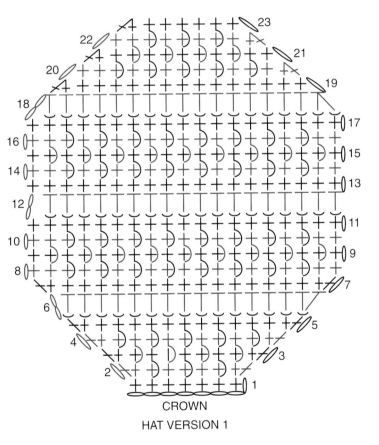

CROWN
HAT VERSION 1

ROW 9: With A, ch 1, sc in first sc, ★sc in next sc, Ssc2 in next sc; rep from ★ across to within last 2 sts, sc in ea of last 2 sc, turn. Drop A, join B.

ROW 10: With B, ch 1, sc in first sc, ★Ssc2 in next sc, sc in next sc; rep from ★ across, turn. Drop B, join A.

ROW 11: Rep row 9. Drop A, join B.

ROW 12: With B, ch 2 (counts as hdc), skip first sc, FLhdc in each sc across, turn. Drop B, join A.

ROW 13: With A, ch 1, sc in each hdc across, sc in top of tch, turn. Drop A, join B.

ROWS 14–17: Rep rows 8–11. Drop A, join B.

ROW 18: With B, ch 2, skip first sc, FLhdc in next sc (counts as first FLhdc2tog), FLhdc in ea sc across to within last 2 sts, FLhdc2tog in last 2 sts, turn—17 sts. Drop B, join A.

ROW 19: With A, ch 1, sk first hdc, sc in ea hdc across to within last 2 hdc and tch, sc2tog over next 2 hdc, turn—15 sts. Drop A, join B.

ROW 20: With B, ch 1, skip first st, sc in ea sc across to within last 2 sts, sc2tog worked across last 2 sts, turn—13 sts. Drop B, join A.

ROW 21: With A, ch 1, sk first st, ★sc in next sc, Ssc2 in next sc, rep from ★ to last within 2 sts, sc2tog worked across last 2 sts, turn—11 sts. Drop A, join B.

ROW 22: With B, ch 1, skip first st, ★sc in next st, Ssc2 in next sc; rep from ★ across to within last 2 sts, sc2tog worked across last 2 sts, turn—13 sts. Drop B, join A.

ROW 23: Rep row 20—7 sts. End off B. Do not cut A, place a safety pin on lp. Steam and gently stretch into a well-formed circle.

SIDES

Note: Sides are worked in joined rounds, turning at the end of each round.

RND 1 (RS): Pick up dropped lp of A at end of last row, ★work 23 sc evenly spaced across left side edge, end off. Tie on A at opposite end of row 1 and work 23 sc evenly spaced across right side edge, change to B.

RND 2 (WS): With B, ch 2 (counts as first hdc), work FLhdc into ea sc around, change to A, sl st in top of beg ch-2 to join, turn.

RND 3: With A, ch 1, sc in ea hdc around, change to B, sl st in first sc to join, turn.

RND 4: With B, ch 1, sc in ea sc around, change to A, sl st in first sc to join, turn.

RND 5: With A, ch 1, sc in next sc, ★Ssc2 in next st, sc in next sc; rep from ★ around, ending with Ssc2 in last st, change to B, sl st in first sc to join, turn.

RND 6: With B, ch 1, sc in next sc, ★Ssc2 in next st, sc in next sc; rep from ★ around, ending with Ssc2 in last st, change to A, sl st in first sc to join, turn.

RND 7: With A, ch 1, sc in next sc, ★Ssc V in next sc, sc in next sc; rep from ★ around, change to B, sl st in first sc to join, turn.

RNDS 8–9: Rep rnds 6–7.

RNDS 10–17: Rep rnds 2–9. End off.

This project was crocheted with:
Lion Brand Yarn's Woolease worsted weight yarn, 80% acrylic, 20% wool, 3oz/85g = 196yd/180m,

(A) 1 skein, Black (153)

(B) 1 skein, Wheat (402)

marguerite

SKILL LEVEL: Easy

FINISHED MEASUREMENTS

Head circumference 19"/48cm

Diameter of top of hat = 7"/18cm

MATERIALS AND TOOLS

Color A: 100yd/92m  DK weight yarn in gold

Color B: 100yd/92m  DK weight yarn in rust

G/6 (4mm) crochet hook or size to obtain gauge

GAUGE

13 sts in patt = 4"/10cm; 7 rows in patt = 1¼"/3cm

16 rows on side of hat = 3"/8cm

Always take time to check your gauge.

CROWN

Note: On all rows with color A (odd-numbered rows in increase section), first and last spike sts are worked as Ssc2 in top of sc 2 rows below, others are worked into the "V" of prev spike 2 rows below. When working these stitches, the V to be worked into is slightly to the left.

With A, ch 8.

ROW 1 (RS): Sc in 2nd ch from hook and in ea ch across—7 sc. Drop A, join B.

ROW 2: With B, ch 1, 2 sc in first sc, sc in ea sc across, 2 sc in last sc—9 sc. Drop B, join A.

ROW 3: With A, ch 1, 2 sc in first sc, sc in next sc, ★Ssc2 in next st, sc in next sc; rep from ★ across, ending with 2 sc in last sc—11 sts. Drop A, join B.

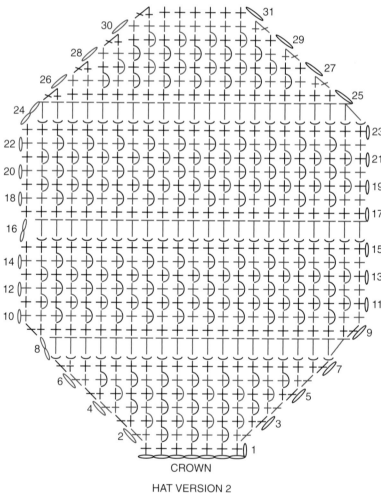

CROWN

HAT VERSION 2

ROW 4: With B, ch 1, 2 sc in first sc, sc in next sc, ★Ssc2 in next sc, sc in next sc; rep from ★ across, ending with 2 sc in last sc, turn—13 sts. Drop B, join A.

ROWS 5-7: Rep rows 3–4; then rep row 3—19 sts at end of last row. Drop A, join B.

ROW 8: With B, ch 2 (counts as hdc), FLhdc in first sc, FLhdc in ea sc across, 2 FLhdc in last sc, turn—21 hdc. Drop B, join A.

ROW 9: With A, ch 1, 2 sc in first hdc, sc in ea hdc across, ending with 2 sc in top of tch—23 sc. Drop A, join B.

ROW 10: With B, ch 1, sc in ea sc across, turn. Drop B, join A.

ROW 11: With A, ch 1, sc in first sc, ★sc in next sc, Ssc2 in next sc; rep from ★ across to within last 2 sts, sc in ea of last 2 sc, turn. Drop A, join B.

ROW 12: With B, ch 1, sc in first sc, ★Ssc2 in next sc, sc in next sc; rep from ★ across, turn. Drop B, join A.

ROWS 13-15: Rep rows 11–12; then rep row 11. Drop A, join B.

ROW 16: With B, ch 2 (counts as hdc), skip first sc, FLhdc in each sc across, turn. Drop B, join A.

ROW 17: With A, ch 1, sc in each hdc across, sc in top of tch, turn. Drop A, join B.

ROWS 18-23: Rep rows 10–15. Drop A, join B.

ROW 24: With B, ch 2, skip first sc, FLhdc in next sc (counts as first FLhdc2tog), FLhdc in ea sc across to within last 2 sts, FLhdc2tog in last 2 sts, turn—21 sts. Drop B, join A.

ROW 25: With A, ch 1, sk first hdc, sc in ea hdc across to within last 2 hdc and tch, sc2tog over next 2 hdc, turn, leaving rem tch unworked—19 sts. Drop A, join B.

ROW 26: With B, ch 1, sk first hdc, sc in ea sc across to within last 2 sc, sc2tog over next 2 sc, turn—17 sts. Drop B, join A.

ROW 27: With A, ch 1, skip first st, ★sc in next st, Ssc2 in next sc; rep from ★ across to within last 2 sts, sc2tog worked across last 2 sts, turn—15 sts. Drop A, join B.

ROW 28: With B, ch 1, sk first st, ★sc in next sc, Ssc2 in next sc, rep from ★ to within last 2 sts, sc2tog worked across last 2 sts, turn—13 sts. Drop B, join A.

ROWS 29-30: Rep rows 27–28—7 sts at end of last row. End off B. Do not cut A, place a safety pin on lp. Steam and gently stretch into a well-formed circle.

SIDES

Note: Sides are worked in joined rnds, turning at the end of each rnd.

RND 1 (RS): Pick up dropped lp of A at end of last row, ★work 25 sc evenly spaced across left side edge, end off. Tie on A at opposite end of row 1 and work 25 sc evenly spaced across right side edge, change to B.

RND 2 (WS): With B, ch 2 (counts as first hdc), skip first sc, work FLhdc into ea sc around, change to A, sl st in top of beg ch-2 to join, turn—64 sc.

RND 3: With A, ch 1, sc in ea hdc around, change to B, sl st in first sc to join, turn. Rnd 4: With B, ch 1, sc in ea sc around, change to A, sl st in first sc to join, turn. Rnd 5: With A, ch 1, sc in first sc, ★Ssc2 in next st, sc in next sc; rep from ★ around, ending with Ssc2 in last st, change to B, sl st in first sc to join, turn.

RND 6: With B, ch 1, sc in first sc, ★Ssc2 in next st, sc in next sc; rep from ★ around, ending with Ssc2 in last st, change to A, sl st in first sc to join, turn.

RND 7: With A, ch 1, sc in first sc, ★Ssc V in next sc, sc in next sc; rep from ★ around, change to B, sl st in first sc to join, turn.

RNDS 8-9: Rep rnds 6–7.

RNDS 10-25: Rep rnds 2–9 twice. End off.

This project was crocheted with:
Berroco Softwist worsted weight yarn ⟨3⟩, 41% wool, 59% rayon, 1.75oz/50g = 100yd/92m

(A) 1 skein, Palmetto (9412)

(B) 1 skein, Incense (9414)

elvira & anna

This last project is an ambitious one, a Tunisian Simple Stitch jacket made with two worsted weights that couldn't be more different: Elvira, a self-striping wool/acrylic, and a fuzzy mohair/linen in a not-quite-solid color, which I call Anna.

The drape of Tunisian Simple Stitch, when worked with a large hook, delights me. The forward pass creates a series of loops held on the long shaft of the Tunisian hook, and on the return pass, a row of chain stitches is run through those loops. What you have then are successive rows of chains held in place by loops running perpendicular to them. There's nothing like that in regular crochet, and I believe this is what accounts for the excellent drape.

I'm also a great fan of Tunisian Simple Stitch (TSS) because the vertical bars create a woven look that's attractive and unusual. TSS takes perfectly to shaping because the stitches are relatively small compared to anything other than single crochet stitches—but single crochet are too small and tight to use in garments, where drape is needed. With smaller stitches, you can create very nice shaping at crucial areas like the armhole, sleeve cap, and collar, and create a beautifully fitting garment. What kinds of yarns will work with TSS? A great many, including some novelties. The only effect I don't care for is a highly textured yarn, which provides no definition for the vertical bars. To my eye, that's the defining element I want to see in Tunisian fabric.

On the other hand, it's a fantastic choice for self-striping yarn, as you can see in Elvira. The normal striping gains considerable complexity, because you get one color in the forward pass of a row and a different one on the return. In other words, instead of solid stripes, a changing kaleidoscope of colors is created. With this particularly yarn, which has harmonious colors and one stronger color—the lime—it really pops out.

In Anna, the mohair/linen blend yarn has three distinct strands in brown, white, and charcoal. The mohair itself is brown and fairly fuzzy, and that color dominates. This blend was chosen over a strictly mohair yarn, where too much fuzz blurred the stitch definition entirely, and the woven look of TSS was lost. The thin strand of linen in this blend provides subtle textural contrast and adds sturdiness to the fabric. The feel of this fabric is divine—soft and buttery—a pleasure against the skin. The fuzz of the mohair led to larger stitches, even though the same size hook was used as in Elvira, and therefore the gauge is different. I wouldn't want to force this yarn into a tighter gauge; the individual stitches need breathing room. When I look at the two versions side by side, one feels stimulating and active, the other calm. It's nice to ponder wearing each on a day when my energy feels different.

elvira

SKILL LEVEL: Intermediate

SIZES
S (M, L, XL)

FINISHED MEASUREMENTS
Bust 37 (41, 45, 50)"/94 (104, 114.5, 127)cm

Length 27 (27 1/2, 28, 28 1/2)"/69 (70, 71, 73)cm

MATERIALS AND TOOLS
1200 (1340, 1500, 1690)yd/1098 (1226, 1372, 1546) m worsted weight wool/acrylic blend yarn in blue/green/gray, **(4)**

K/10½ (6.5mm) Afghan crochet hook or size to obtain gauge

K/10½ (6.5mm) standard crochet hook

J/10 (6mm) standard crochet hook

Yarn needle

Sewing needle and matching sewing thread

5 buttons 1"/3cm in diameter

GAUGE
12 sts and 12 rows in TSS = 4"/10cm

Always take time to check your gauge.

SPECIAL STITCHES
Tunisian Simple Stitch (TSS): Row 1 *forward pass:* Working in BL of ch sts, insert hook in 2nd ch from hook, yo and draw up a lp, ★keeping all lps on hook, insert hook in next ch, yo and draw up a lp; rep from ★ across. Row 1 *return pass:* Yo and draw lp through first lp on hook, ★yo and draw through 2 lps on hook; rep from ★ across. You will have one lp on the hook at the end and it will count as first st of next row. Pull working yarn firmly before starting next forward pass, to eliminate excess yarn in this lp.

Row 2 forward pass: Skip the first vertical bar, ★insert hook under next vertical bar, yo, draw lp through keeping lp on hook; rep from ★ across, ending by inserting hook under 2 strands of last vertical bar, yo, draw lp through to make firmer edge. Row 2 *return pass:* Rep return pass of row 1.

Increasing: Increasing is done in the forward pass. To increase 1 st at the end of the row: Insert hook

between the last 2 vertical bars (under the top 2 lps of the horizontal chain), draw lp through, work last lp under 2 strands as usual.

To increase 1 st at the beg of a row: Sk first vertical bar as usual, ★pick up the next lp by inserting hook between the 1st and 2nd vertical bars (under the top 2 lps of the horizontal chain). Pick up the next bar as usual and cont across row as usual. Note: To eliminate a "hole," be sure to insert hook under 2 lps only.

To increase 2 sts at the beg of a forward pass: Ch 1 (after completing return pass), draw up a lp in first vertical bar (1-st inc), pick up the next lp by inserting hook between the 1st and 2nd vertical bars (under the top 2 lps of the horizontal chain). Pick up the next bar as usual and cont across row as usual.

Decreasing: Decreasing is usually done in the forward pass as follows: Dec st at the end of the row: Insert hook under both 2nd to last and last vertical bars, yo and draw through both lps. Dec 2 sts at the end of the row: Insert hook under last 3 vertical bars, yo and draw through all 3 lps.

Note: You will find some decreases done in the return pass in this pattern as follows. This is done because the result is more attractive.

Dec 1 st at beg of row (worked on Sleeve): This will actually be done at the end of the return pass. Work until there are 3 lps on hook, yo, pull through all 3 lps. On next forward pass, treat these gathered lps at the beg of the row as 1 vertical bar.

Dec 2 st at beg of row (worked on Sleeve): This will be done on return pass of row. Work until there are 4 lps on hook, yo, pull through all 4 lps. On next forward pass, treat these gathered lps at the beg of the row as 1 vertical bar.

Slip stitch end off (sl st end off): ★Insert hook under next vertical bar, draw lp through vertical bar and the lp on the hook at the same time; rep from ★ across, always having 1 lp on the hook, ending by inserting hook under 2 strands of last st, yo, draw lp through vertical bar and lp on hook. End off.

Note: All pieces are worked in vertical rows.

BACK

Starting at left side edge, ch 53.

ROW 1: Work in TSS across—53 sts.

FIRST ARMHOLE SHAPING

ROWS 2–6 (2–8, 2–9, 2–11): Work in TSS, inc 1 st at the end of the forward pass—58 (60, 61, 63) sts at end of last row. Tie on a separate strand at end of row and with standard K hook, ch 19 (19, 20, 20) for straight part of armhole. End off strand.

ROW 7 (9, 10, 12): Work forward pass over previous row and added chains—77 (79, 81, 83) sts.

SHOULDER SLOPE SHAPING

Cont working in TSS for a total of 20 (23, 25, 28) rows, inc 1 st at end of the following rows: 8–12–16–20 (10–14–18–23, 11–15–20–25, 13–18–23–28)—81 (83, 85, 87) sts at end of last row.

NECK SHAPING

ROWS 21–22 (24–25, 26–27, 29–31): Work in TSS, dec 1 st at end of row—79 (81, 83, 84) sts at end of last row.

ROWS 23–33 (26–37, 28–41, 32–44): Work even in TSS.

ROWS 34–35 (38–39, 42–43, 45–47): Inc 1 st at end of row—81 (83, 85, 87) sts at end of last row.

SECOND SHOULDER

ROWS 36–49 (40–54, 44–59, 48–64): Cont working in TSS, dec 1 st at end of the following rows: 36–40–44–48 (40–45–49–53, 44–49–54–59, 48–53–58–63)—77 (79, 81, 83) sts at end of last row.

SECOND ARMHOLE SHAPING

ROW 50 (55, 60, 65): Work forward pass for 58 (60, 61, 63) sts. Leaving sts on hook and beg on next st, work sl st in each st to end. Cut yarn. With cut end of skein, yo and draw through 2 lps on hook to begin return pass row, work return pass row across—57 (59, 60, 62) sts at end of return pass.

ROWS 51–54 (56–61, 61–67, 66–74): Work in TSS, dec 1 st at end of row—53 sts at end of last row.

Work 2 rows even in TSS. Work sl st end off.

FRONT RIGHT

Work same as for Back through row 20 (23, 25, 28)—81 (83, 85, 87) sts at end of last row.

NECKLINE SHAPING

ROW 21 (24, 26, 29): Work in TSS until there are 5 vertical bars left, insert hook under next 2 vertical bars and pull lp through (1-st dec made), leave rem sts unworked (4-st dec total), work return pass—77 (79, 81, 83) sts.

ROW 22 (25, 27, 30): Work in TSS until there are 3 vertical bars left, insert hook under all 3 vertical bars and pull lp through (2-st dec made)—75 (77, 79, 81) sts.

ROWS 23–28 (26–32, 28–35, 31–38): Work even in TSS.

BUTTONHOLES

ROW 29 (33, 36, 39): Forward pass: Pick up a st in first 10 (11, 10, 11) bars, ★sl st over next 2 bars, pick up 11 (11, 12, 12) bars; rep from ★ 3 times, sl st over next 2 bars, pick up ea of last 11 (12, 11, 12) vertical bars. Return pass: Work return pass as usual until first buttonhole, ★ch 2 over buttonhole, bringing 2nd ch through next vertical bar, cont return pass until next buttonhole; rep from ★ to end.

ROW 30 (34, 37, 40): Pick up vertical bar in ea vertical bar to first buttonhole, ★pick up vertical bar in BL of ea of next 2 ch, pick up ea vertical bar until next buttonhole; rep from ★ to end, work return pass as usual.

ROW 31 (35, 38, 41): Work TSS across. Work sl st end off. Do not cut yarn.

NECKLINE SHAPING

ROW 21 (24, 26, 29): Sl st over first 3 sts, insert hook under next 2 vertical bars and draw up lp (1-st dec), work in TSS to end, work return pass—77 (79, 81, 83) sts.

ROW 22 (25, 27, 30): Work forward pass across. Return pass: Work in TSS until there are 3 lps on hook, pull final lp thru both lps (2-st dec at beg of row)—75 (77, 79, 81) sts.

ROWS 23–31 (26–35, 28–38, 31–41): Work even in TSS. Work sl st end off, cut yarn.

SLEEVE (MAKE 2)
Ch 50.

ROW 1: Work even in TSS.

ROWS 2–6 (2–8, 2–9, 2–11): Work in TSS, inc 1 st at beg of row—55 (57, 58, 60) sts at end of last row.

ROWS 7–12 (9–14, 10–15, 12–17): Work in TSS, inc 2 sts at beg of row—67 (69, 70, 72) sts at end of last row.

ROWS 13–16 (15–18, 16–19, 18–21): Work in TSS, inc 1 st at beg of row—71 (73, 74, 76) sts at end of last row.

ROWS 17–24 (19–26, 20–29, 22–32): Work even in TSS.

ROWS 25–28 (27–30, 30–33, 33–36): Work in TSS, dec 1 st at beg of row—67 (69, 70, 72) sts at end of last row.

ROWS 29–34 (31–36, 34–39, 37–42): Work in TSS, dec 2 sts at beg of row—55 (57, 58, 60) sts at end of last row.

FRONT LEFT
Starting at left side edge, ch 53.

ROW 1: Work in TSS across—53 sts.

FIRST ARMHOLE SHAPING

ROWS 2–6 (2–8, 2–9, 2–11): Work in TSS, inc 1 st at the beg of the forward pass—58 (60, 61, 63) sts at end of last row. At end of last row, ch 20 (20, 21, 21) for straight part of armhole.

ROW 7 (9, 10, 12): Work forward pass over added chains, then over previous row—77 (79, 81, 83) sts.

SHOULDER SLOPE SHAPING
Cont working in TSS for a total of 20 (23, 25, 28) rows, inc 1 st at beg of the following rows: 8–12–16–20 (10–14–18–23, 11–15–20–25, 13–18–23–28)—81 (83, 85, 87) sts at end of last row.

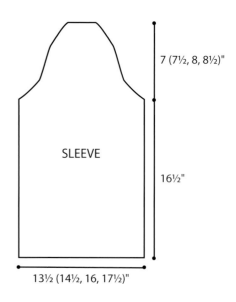

7 (7½, 8, 8½)"

SLEEVE

16½"

13½ (14½, 16, 17½)"

ROWS 35–39 (37–43, 41–48, 43–52): Work in TSS, dec 1 st at beg of row—50 sts at end of last row. Work sl st end off, cut yarn.

FINISHING

Weave in all ends with yarn needle. Steam all pieces flat. Sew side and shoulder seams from WS with mattress stitch. Work shoulder seams twice to strengthen. Sew sleeves to armholes from WS with mattress stitch. Sew sleeve seams.

COLLAR

Using yarn from front right, with J standard hook and RS facing, work evenly spaced sc around neckline, sl st to corner st at top of last row on front left, end off. Make sure there are the same number of sts from each front piece to the shoulder.

ROW 1: With WS facing, count 4 sc from left edge. With Tunisian hook, insert hook into top of this st and pick up lp. Cont picking up lps in ea sc, ending by working into 4th sc from right edge. Work return pass as usual.

Work 11 more rows even for collar.

FINISHING

Sew buttons to left front opposite buttonholes. Steam collar flat.

> **This project was crocheted with:**
> 12 (14, 15, 17) balls Trendsetter Tonalita worsted weight yarn (**4**), 52% wool, 48% acrylic, 1.75oz/50g = 100yd/92m, in Army/Navy (2418)

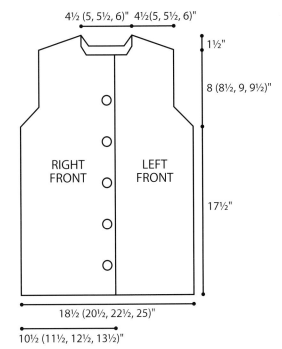

4½ (5, 5½, 6)" 4½(5, 5½, 6)"

1½"

8 (8½, 9, 9½)"

RIGHT FRONT   LEFT FRONT

17½"

18½ (20½, 22½, 25)"

10½ (11½, 12½, 13½)"

anna

SKILL LEVEL: Intermediate

SIZES
S (M, L, XL)

FINISHED MEASUREMENTS
Bust 37 (41, 45, 50)"/94 (104, 114.5, 127)cm

Length 27 (27 1/2, 28, 28 1/2)"/69 (70, 71, 73)cm

MATERIALS AND TOOLS
1000 (1200, 1300, 1450)yd/915 (1098,1189,1326)m light worsted weight mohair blend yarn in brown,

K/10½ (6.5mm) Afghan crochet hook or size to obtain gauge

K/10½ (6.5mm) standard crochet hook

J/10 (6mm) standard crochet hook

Yarn needle

Sewing needle and matching sewing thread

5 buttons 1"/3cm in diameter

GAUGE
11 sts and 12 rows in TSS = 4"/10cm

Always take time to check your gauge.

SPECIAL STITCHES

Tunisian Simple Stitch (TSS): Row 1 forward pass: Working in BL of ch sts, insert hook in 2nd ch from hook, yo and draw up a lp, ★keeping all lps on hook, insert hook in next ch, yo and draw up a lp; rep from ★ across. Row 1 return pass: Yo and draw lp through first lp on hook, ★yo and draw through 2 lps on hook; rep from ★ across. You will have one lp on the hook at the end and it will count as first st of next row. Pull working yarn firmly before starting next forward pass, to eliminate excess yarn in this lp.

Row 2 forward pass: Skip the first vertical bar, ★insert hook under next vertical bar, yo, draw lp through keeping lp on hook; rep from ★ across, ending by inserting hook under 2 strands of last vertical bar, yo, draw lp through to make firmer edge. Row 2 return pass: Rep return pass of row 1.

Increasing: Increasing is done in the forward pass. To increase 1 st at the end of the row: Insert hook between the last 2 vertical bars (under the top 2 lps of the horizontal chain), draw lp through, work last lp under 2 strands as usual.

To increase 1 st at the beg of a row: Sk first vertical bar as usual, ★pick up the next lp by inserting hook between the 1st and 2nd vertical bars (under the top 2 lps of the horizontal chain). Pick up the next bar as usual and cont across row as usual.

Note: To eliminate a "hole," be sure to insert hook under 2 lps only.

To increase 2 sts at the beg of a forward pass: Ch 1 (after completing return pass), draw up a lp in first vertical bar (1 st inc), pick up the next lp by inserting hook between the 1st and 2nd vertical bars (under the top 2 lps of the horizontal chain). Pick up the next bar as usual and cont across row as usual.

Decreasing: Decreasing is usually done in the forward pass as follows: Dec 1 st at the end of the row: Insert hook under both 2nd to last and last vertical bars, yo and draw through lp.

Note: You will find some decreases done in the return pass in this pattern as follows. This is done because the result is more attractive.

Dec 1 st at beg of row (worked on Sleeve): This will actually be done at the end of the return pass. Work until there are 3 lps on hook, yo, pull through all 3 lps. On next forward pass, treat these gathered lps at the beg of the row as 1 vertical bar.

Dec 2 st at beg of row (worked on Sleeve): This will be done on return pass of row. Work until there are 4 lps on hook, yo, pull through all 4 lps. On next forward pass, treat these gathered lps at the beg of the row as 1 vertical bar.

Slip stitch end off (sl st end off): ★Insert hook under next vertical bar, draw lp through vertical bar and the lp on the hook at the same time; rep from ★ across, always having 1 lp on the hook, ending by inserting hook under 2 strands of last st, yo, draw lp through vertical bar and lp on hook. End off.

Note: All pieces are worked in vertical rows.

BACK

Starting at left side edge, ch 50.

ROW 1: Work in TSS across—50 sts.

FIRST ARMHOLE SHAPING

ROWS 2–6 (2-8, 2--9, 2-11): Work in TSS, inc 1 st at the end of the forward pass—55 (57, 58, 60) sts at end of last row. Tie on a separate strand at end of row and with standard K hook, ch 17 (17, 18, 18) for straight part of armhole. End off strand.

ROW 7 (9, 10, 12): Work forward pass over previous row and added chains—72 (74, 76, 78) sts.

SHOULDER SLOPE SHAPING

Cont working in TSS for a total of 20 (23, 25, 28) rows, inc 1 st at end of the following rows: 8–12–16–20 (10–14–18–23, 11–15–20–25, 13–18–23–28)—76 (78, 80, 82) sts at end of last row.

NECK SHAPING

ROWS 21–22 (24-25, 26-27, 29-31): Work in TSS, dec 1 st at end of row—74 (76, 78, 79) sts at end of last row.

ROWS 23–33 (26-37, 28-41, 32-44): Work even in TSS.

ROWS 34–35 (38-39, 42-43, 45-47): Inc 1 st at end of row—76 (78, 80, 82) sts at end of last row.

SECOND SHOULDER

ROWS 36–49 (40-54, 44-59, 48-64): Cont working in TSS, dec **1 ST AT END OF THE FOLLOWING ROWS:** 36–40–44–48 (40–45–49–53, 44–49–54–59, 48–53–58–63)—76 (78, 80, 82) sts at end of last row.

SECOND ARMHOLE SHAPING

ROW 50 (55, 60, 65): Work forward pass for 55 (57, 58, 60) sts. Leaving sts on hook and beg on next st, work sl st in each st to end. Cut yarn. With cut end of skein, yo and draw through 2 lps on hook to begin return pass row, work return pass row across—54 (56, 57, 59) sts at end of return pass.

ROWS 51–54 (56-61, 61-67, 66-74): Work in TSS, dec 1 st at end of row—50 sts at end of last row.

Work 2 rows even in TSS. Work sl st end off.

FRONT RIGHT

Work same as Back through row 20 (23, 25, 28)—76 (78, 80, 82) sts at end of last row.

NECKLINE SHAPING

ROW 21 (24, 26, 29): Work in TSS until there are 5 vertical bars left, insert hook under next 2 vertical bars and pull lp through, leave rem sts unworked (4-st dec total), work return pass—72 (74, 76, 78) sts.

ROW 22 (25, 27, 30): Work in TSS until there are 3 vertical bars left, insert hook under all 3 vertical bars and pull lp through (2-st dec made)—70 (72, 74, 76) sts.

ROWS 23–28 (26–32, 28–35, 31–38): Work even in TSS.

BUTTONHOLES

ROW 29 (33, 36, 39): Forward pass: Pick up a st in first 8 (9, 8, 9) bars, ★sl st over next 2 bars, pick up 11 (11, 12, 12) bars; rep from ★ 3 times, sl st over next 2 bars, pick up ea of last 8 (9, 8, 9) vertical bars. Return pass: Work return pass as usual until first buttonhole, ★ch 2 over buttonhole, bringing 2nd ch through next vertical bar, cont return pass until next buttonhole; rep from ★ to end.

ROW 30 (34, 37, 40): Pick up vertical bar in ea vertical bar to first buttonhole, ★pick up vertical bar in BL of ea of next 2 ch, pick up ea vertical bar until next buttonhole; rep from ★ to end. Work return pass as usual.

ROW 31 (35, 38, 41): Work TSS across. Work sl st end off. Do not cut yarn.

FRONT LEFT

Starting at left side edge, ch 50.

ROW 1: Work in TSS across—50 sts.

FIRST ARMHOLE SHAPING

ROWS 2–6 (2–8, 2–9, 2–11): Work in TSS, inc 1 st at the beg of the forward pass—58 (60, 61, 63) sts at end of last row. At end of last row, ch 18 (18, 19, 19) for straight part of armhole.

ROW 7 (9, 10, 12): Work forward pass over added chains, then over previous row—72 (74, 76, 78) sts.

SHOULDER SLOPE SHAPING

Cont working in TSS for a total of 20 (23, 25, 28) rows, inc 1 st at beg of the following rows: 8–12–16–20 (10–14–18–23, 11–15–20–25, 13–18–23–28)—76 (78, 80, 82) sts at end of last row.

NECKLINE SHAPING

ROW 21 (24, 26, 29): Sl st over first 3 sts, insert hook under next 2 vertical bars and draw up lp, work in TSS to end, work return pass—72 (74, 76, 78) sts.

ROW 22 (25, 27, 30): Work forward pass across. Return pass: Work in TSS until there are 3 lps on hook, pull final lp through both lps (2-st dec at beg of row)—70 (72, 74, 79) sts.

ROWS 23–31 (26–35, 28–38, 31–41): Work even in TSS. Work sl st end off, cut yarn.

SLEEVE (MAKE 2)

Ch 46.

ROW 1: Work even in TSS.

ROWS 2–6 (2–8, 2–9, 2–11): Work in TSS, inc 1 st at beg of row—51 (53, 54, 56) sts at end of last row.

ROWS 7–12 (9–14, 10–15, 12–17): Work in TSS, inc 2 sts at beg of row—63 (65, 66, 68) sts at end of last row.

ROWS 13–16 (15–18, 16–19, 18–21): Work in TSS, inc 1 st at beg of row—67 (69, 70, 72) sts at end of last row.

ROWS 17–24 (19–26, 20–29, 22–32): Work even in TSS.

ROWS 25–28 (27–30, 30–33, 33–36): Work in TSS, dec 1 st at beg of row—63 (65, 66, 68) sts at end of last row.

ROWS 29–34 (31–36, 34–39, 37–42): Work in TSS, dec 2 sts at beg of row—51 (53, 54, 56) sts at end of last row.

ROWS 35–39 (37–43, 41–47, 43–52): Work in TSS, dec 1 st at beg of row—46 sts at end of last row.

ROW 40 (44, 48, 53): Work even in TSS. Work sl st end off, cut yarn.

FINISHING

Weave in all ends with yarn needle. Steam all pieces flat.

SEAMS

The yarn used in this model combined with the natural curl of Tunisian crochet made seams worked from the inside problematic. Side seams, armhole seams, and sleeve seams were all worked from the outside with whipstitch over the outermost loops. Two stitches were worked in each edge stitch. This produces a visible surface that adds a nice design element. It also leaves a gap between the seam and the body of the garment. To fill in this gap, weave a strand from WS of garment back and forth over this space. Shoulder seams were sewn from WS using running stitch.

COLLAR

Using yarn from front right, with J standard hook and RS facing, work evenly spaced sc around neckline, sl st to corner st at top of last row on front left, end off. Make sure there are the same number of stitches from each front piece to the shoulder.

ROW 1: With WS facing, count 4 sc from left edge. With Tunisian hook, insert hook into top of this st and pick up lp. Cont picking up lps in ea sc, ending by working into 4th sc from right edge. Work return pass as usual.

Work 11 more rows even for collar.

FINISHING

Sew buttons to left front opposite buttonholes. Steam collar flat.

This project was crocheted with:
9 (10, 11, 12) skeins Louet Kidlin light worsted weight yarn (**4**), 53% kid mohair, 24% linen, 23% nylon, 1.75oz/150g = 120yd/110m, in Toasted Coconut (77)

Stitch Dictionary

Puffs & Crosses

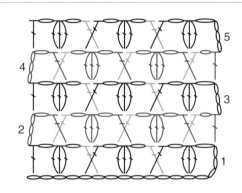

Chain multiples of 5 plus 3.

3-DC PUFF ST: (Yo, insert hook in next st, yo, draw yarn through st, yo, draw yarn through 2 loops on hook) 3 times in same st, yo, draw yarn through 4 loops on hook.

ROW 1 (RS): 3-dc puff st in 6th ch from hook, *ch 1, sk next 2 ch, dc in next ch, working behind last dc made, dc in last skipped ch (crossed dc made), ch 1, sk next ch, 3-dc puff st in next ch; rep from * across to within last 2 ch, ch 1, sk next ch, dc in last ch, turn.

ROW 2: Ch 4 (counts as dc, ch 1), *sk next ch-1 sp, dc in next ch-1 sp, working behind last dc made, dc in last skipped ch-1 sp (crossed dc made), ch 1**, 3-dc puff st between next 2 dc, ch 1; rep from * across, ending last rep at**, dc in next ch of tch, turn.

ROW 3: Ch 4 (counts as dc, ch 1), sk next ch-1 sp, *3-dc puff st between next 2 dc, ch 1, sk next ch-1 sp**, dc in next ch-1 sp, working behind last dc made, dc in last skipped ch-1 sp (crossed dc made), ch 1; rep from * across, ending last rep at**, dc in 3rd ch of tch, turn.

Rep rows 2-3 for patt.

Sidesaddle Shell

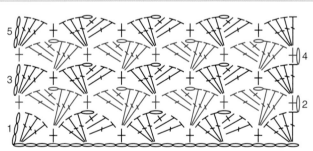

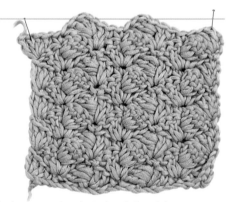

Chain a multiple of 6 plus 4.

ROW 1 (WS): 3 dc in 4th ch from hook, *sk next 2 ch, sc in next ch, sk next 2 ch**, 3 dc in next ch, ch 1, (sc, hdc, dc) around the post of last dc made; rep from * across, ending last rep at **, 4 dc in last ch, turn.

ROW 2: Ch 1, sc in first sc, *sk next 3 dc, 3 dc in next sc, ch 1, (sc, hdc, dc) around the post of last dc made, sk next 3 sts, sc in next ch-1 sp; rep from * acrossending with last sc in top of tch, turn.

ROW 3: Ch 3 (counts as dc), 3 dc in first sc, *sk next 3 sts, sc in next ch-1 sp, sk next 3 sts**, 3 dc in next sc, ch 1, (sc, hdc, dc) around the post of last dc made; rep from * across, ending last rep at **, 4 dc in last sc, turn.

Rep rows 2-3 for patt.

 Roundels

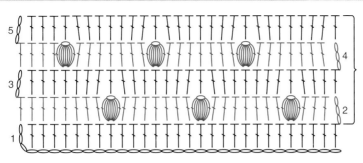

Roundel: Work (dc, ch 2) 9 times in designated st, remove hook, fold roundel down to front, insert hook from front to back in first dc of roundel, pull dropped lp through.

Chain a multiple of 8 plus 5, plus 2.

ROW 1 (WS): Dc in 4th ch from hook and in ea ch across, turn.

ROW 2 (RS): Ch 3 (counts as dc), dc in ea of next 3 dc, ★roundel in next dc, dc in ea of next 7 sts; rep from ★ across, ending with dc in top of tch, turn.

ROW 3: Ch 3, dc in ea st across (working 1 dc in ea roundel), dc in top of tch, turn.

ROW 4: Ch 3, ★dc in ea of next 7 dc, roundel in next dc; rep from ★ across, ending with dc in last 3 dc, dc in top of tch, turn.

ROW 5: Ch 3, dc in ea dc across, dc in top of tch, turn.

Rep rows 2-5 for patt.

 Roundel variation

Roundel: 12 dc in same st, fold roundel down to front, insert hook from front to back in first dc of roundel, pull dropped lp through.

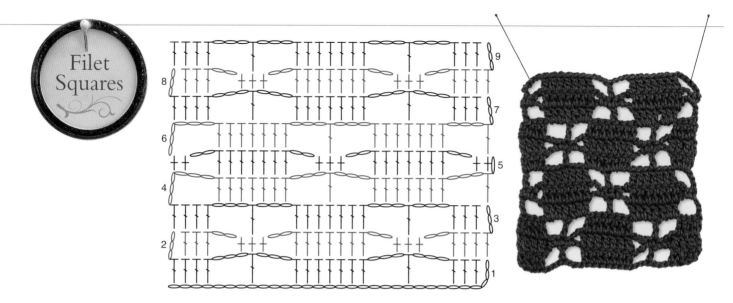

Filet Squares

Chain multiples of 14 plus 3.

ROW 1 (RS): Dc in 4th ch from hook, dc in ea of next 2 ch, ★ch 3, sk next 3 ch, dc in next dc, ch 3, sk next 3 ch★★, dc in ea of next 7 ch; rep from ★ across, ending last rep at ★★, dc in ea of last 4 ch, turn.

ROW 2: Ch 3 (counts as dc), sk first dc, dc in ea of next 3 dc, ★ch 2, sc in next ch-3 sp, sc in next dc, sc in next ch-3 sp, ch 2★★, dc in ea of next 7 dc; rep from ★ across, ending last rep at ★★, dc in ea of next 3 dc, dc in top of tch, turn.

ROW 3: Ch 3 (counts as dc), sk first dc, dc in ea of next 3 dc, ★ch 3, sk next sc, dc in next sc, ch 3, sk next ch-3 sp★★, dc in ea of next 7 dc; rep from ★ across, ending last rep at ★★, dc in ea of next 3 dc, dc in top of tch, turn.

ROW 4: Ch 6 (counts as dc, ch 3), sk first 4 dc, ★3 dc in next ch-3 sp, dc in next dc, 3 dc in next ch-3 sp, ch 3, sk next 3 dc★★, dc in next dc, ch 3, sk next 3 dc; rep from ★ across, ending last rep at ★★, dc in top of tch, turn.

ROW 5: Ch 1, sc in first dc, ★sc in next ch-3 sp, ch 2, 7 dc in ea of next 7 dc, ch 2, sc in next ch-3 sp★★, sc in next dc; rep from ★ across, ending last rep at ★★, sc in 3rd ch of tch, turn.

ROW 6: Ch 6 (counts as dc, ch 3), sk next ch-2 sp, ★dc in ea of next 7 dc, ch 3, sk next sc, dc in next sc★★, ch 3, sk next ch-2 sp; rep from ★ across, ending last rep at ★★, turn.

ROW 7: Ch 3 (counts as dc), sk first dc, 3 dc in next ch-3 sp, ★ch 3, sk next 3 dc, dc in next dc, ch 3, sk next 3 dc, 3 dc in next ch-3 sp★★, dc in next dc; rep from ★ across, ending last rep at ★★, dc in 3rd ch of tch, turn.

Rep rows 2-7 for patt, ending with row 3 or row 6 of patt.

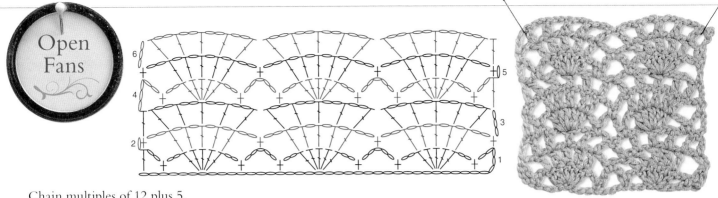

Open Fans

Chain multiples of 12 plus 5.

ROW 1 (RS): Sc in 7th ch from hook, ★ch 2, sk next 3 ch, 5 dc in next ch, ch 2, sk next 3 ch, sc in next ch★★, ch 5, sk next 3 ch, sc in next ch; rep from ★ across, ending last rep at ★★, ch 2, sk next ch, dc in last ch, turn.

ROW 2: Ch 1, sc in first dc, ★ch 2, sk next 2 ch-2 sps, (dc, ch 1) in ea of next 4 dc, dc in next dc, ch 2, sk next ch-2 sp★★, sc in next ch-5 loop; rep from ★ across, ending last rep at ★★, sk next 2 ch, sc in next ch of tch, turn.

ROW 3: Ch 3 (counts as dc), sk next ch-2 sp, ★(dc, ch 2) in ea of next 4 dc, dc in next dc★★, sk next 2 ch-2 sps; rep from ★ across, ending last rep at ★★, sk next ch-2 sp, dc in last sc, turn.

ROW 4: Ch 5 (counts as dc, ch 2), ★sc in next ch-2 sp, ch 2, sk next ch-2 sp, 5 dc in next dc, ch 2, sk next ch-2 sp, sc in next ch-2 sp★★, ch 5; rep from ★ across, ending last rep at ★★, ch 2, dc in 3rd ch of tch, turn.

Rep rows 2-4 for patt.

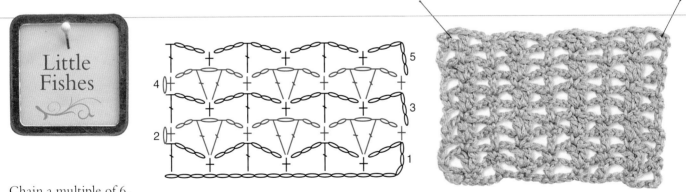

Little Fishes

Chain a multiple of 6.

ROW 1 (RS): Sc in 9th ch from hook, ch 3, sk next 2 ch, dc in next ch, ★ch 3, sk next 2 ch, sc in next ch, ch 3, sk next 2 ch, dc in next ch; rep from ★ across, turn.

ROW 2: Ch 1, sc in first dc, ★ch 2, (dc, ch 1, dc) in next sc, ch 2★★, sc in next dc; rep from ★ across, ending last rep at ★★, sk next 3 ch, sc in next ch of tch, turn.

ROW 3: Ch 6 (counts as dc, ch 3), sk next ch-2 sp, sc in next ch-1 sp, ch 3, sk next ch-2 sp, dc in next sc, ★ch 3, sk next ch-2 sp, sc in next ch-1 sp, ch 3, sk next ch-2 sp, dc in next sc; rep from ★ across, ending with last dc in 3rd ch of tch, turn.

Rep rows 2-3 for patt.

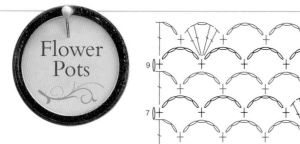

Flower
Pots

Chain a multiple of 24 plus 9 plus 1.

SHELL: (2 dc, ch 1, 2 dc) in same st.

ROW 1 (WS): Sc in 2nd ch from hook, ★ch 5, sk next 3 ch, sc in next ch; rep from ★ across, turn.

ROW 2: Ch 5 (counts as dc, ch 2), ★sc in next ch-5 sp, shell in next sc★★, (sc, ch 5) in ea of next 5 ch-5 sps; rep from ★ across, ending last rep at ★★, sc in next ch-5 sp, ch 2, dc in last sc, turn.

ROW 3: Ch 1, sc in first dc, ★shell in next sc, sc in next ch-1, shell in next sc★★, (sc, ch 5) in ea of next 4 ch-5 sps, sc in next ch-5 sp; rep from ★ across, ending last rep at ★★, sc in 3rd ch of tch, turn.

ROW 4: Ch 5 (counts as dc, ch 2), ★sc in next ch-1 sp, shell in next sc, sc in next ch-1 sp★★, (ch 5, sc) in ea of next 4 ch-5 sps, ch 5; rep from ★ across, ending last rep at ★★, ch 2, dc in last sc, turn.

ROW 5: Ch 1, sc in first dc, ch 5, ★sc in next ch-1 sp, ch 5★★, (sc, ch 5) in ea of next 5 ch-5 sps; rep from ★ across ending last rep at ★★, sc in 3rd ch of tch, turn.

ROW 6: Ch 5 (counts as dc, ch 2), ★(sc, ch 5) in ea of next 3 ch-5 sps, sc in next ch-5 sp, shell in next sc, (sc, ch 5) in ea of next 2 ch-5 sps; rep from ★ across to within last 2 ch-5 sps, sc in next ch-5 sp, ch 5, sc in next ch-5 sp, ch 2, dc in last sc, turn.

ROW 7: Ch 1, sc in first dc, ★(ch 5, sc) in ea of next 3 ch-5 sps, shell in next sc, sc in next ch-1 sp, shell in next ch-5 sp, ch 5, sc in next ch-5 sp; rep from ★ across to within last 2 ch-5 sps, ch 5, sc in next ch-5 sp, ch 5, sc in 3rd ch of tch, turn.

ROW 8: Ch 5 (counts as dc, ch 2), ★(sc, ch 5) in ea of next 3 ch-5 sps, sc in next ch-1 sp, shell in next sc, sc in next ch-1 sp, ch 5; rep from ★ across to within last 3 ch-5 sps, (sc, ch 5) in ea of next 2 ch-5 sps, sc in next ch-5 sp, ch 2, dc in last sc, turn.

ROW 9: Ch 1, sc in first dc, ch 5, ★(sc, ch 5) in ea of next 3 ch-5 sps, sc in next ch-1 sp, ch 5, (sc, ch 5) in ea of next 2 ch-5 sps; rep from ★ across to within last 2 ch-5 sps, sc in next ch-5 sp, ch 5, sc in 3rd ch of tch, turn.

Rep rows 2-9 for patt.

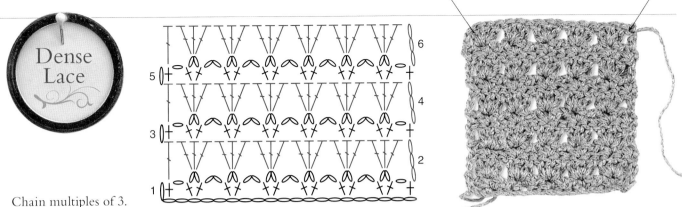

Dense Lace

Chain multiples of 3.

ROW 1 (WS): Sc in 2nd ch from hook, ch 1, sk next ch, (sc, ch 2, sc) in next ch, *ch 2, sk next 2 ch, (sc, ch 2, sc) in next ch; rep from * across to within last 2 ch, ch 1, sk next ch, sc in last ch, turn.

ROW 2: Ch 3 (counts as dc), sk next ch-1 sp, 3 dc in next ch-2 sp, *sk next ch-2 sps, 3 dc in next ch-2 sp; rep from * across to last ch-2 sp, sk next ch-1 sp, dc in last sc, turn.

ROW 3: Ch 1, sc in first dc, ch 1, sk next dc, (sc, ch 2, sc) in next dc, *ch 2, sk next 2 dc, (sc, ch 2, sc) in next dc; rep from * across to within last 2 sts, ch 1, sk next dc, sc in 3rd ch of tch, turn.

Rep rows 2-3 for patt.

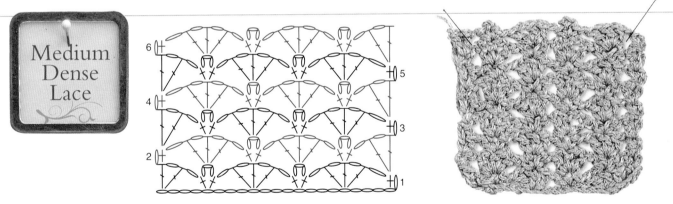

Medium Dense Lace

Chain multiples of 8 plus 6.

ROW 1 (RS): Sc in 2nd ch from hook, *ch 1, sk next 3 ch, (dc, ch 1, dc, ch 1, dc) in next ch, ch 1, sk next 3 ch, (sc, ch 3, sc) in next ch; rep from * across to within last 4 ch, ch 1, sk next 3 ch, (dc, ch 1, dc) in last ch, turn.

ROW 2: Ch 1, sc in first dc, *ch 1, sk next 2 ch-1 sps, (dc, ch 1, dc, ch 1, dc) in next ch-3 loop, ch 1, sk next 2 ch-1 sps, (sc, ch 3, sc) in next dc; rep from * across to within last 2 ch-1 sps, ch 1, sk next 2 ch-1 sps, (dc, ch 1, dc) in last sc, turn.

Rep row 2 for patt.

Very Open Lace

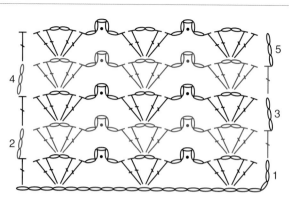

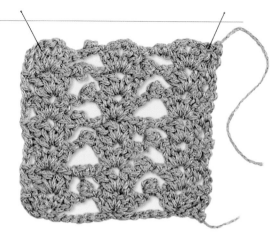

Chain multiples of 7 plus 2.

ROW 1 (RS): (2 dc, ch 2, 2 dc) in 6th ch from hook, *ch 1, ch 3, sl st in 3rd ch from hook (picot), ch 1, sk next 6 ch, (2 dc, ch 2, 2 dc) in next ch; rep from * across to within last 3 ch, sk next 2 ch, dc in last ch, turn.

ROW 2: Ch 3 (counts as dc), sk first 3 dc, (2 dc, ch 2, 2 dc) in next ch–2 sp, *ch 1, picot, ch 1, (2 dc, ch 2, 2 dc) in next ch–2 sp; rep from * across to last ch–2 sp, sk next 2 dc, dc in top of tch, turn.

Rep Row 2 for patt.

Circle of Fans

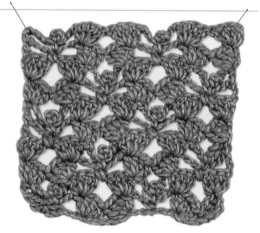

PICOT: Ch 3, sl st in 3rd ch from hook.

Chain multiples of 12 plus 4.

ROW 1 (WS): 3 dc in 4th ch from hook, *sk next 5 ch, 4 dc in next ch, ch 3, sk next 2 ch, sc in next ch, ch 3, sk next 2 ch★★, 4 dc in next ch; rep from * across, ending last rep at ★★, dc in last ch, turn.

ROW 2: Ch 6 (counts as dc, ch 3), sk next ch-3 sp, *sc in next sc, picot, ch 3, sk next ch-3 sp, 4 dc in next dc, sk next 6 dc★★, 4 dc in next dc, ch 3, sk next ch-3 sp; rep from * across, ending last rep at ★★, 4 dc in top of tch, turn.

ROW 3: Ch 6 (counts as dc, ch 3), sk first 4 dc, *sc bet next 2 dc, ch 3, sk next 3 dc, 4 dc in next dc, sk next 2 ch-3 sps★★, 4 dc in next dc, ch 3, sk next 3 dc; rep from * across, ending last rep at ★★, 4 dc in 3rd ch of tch, turn.

ROW 4: Ch 3 (counts as dc), 3 dc in first dc, *sk next 6 dc, 4 dc in next dc, ch 3, sk next ch-3 sp, sc in next sc, picot, ch 3, sk next ch-3 sp★★, 4 dc in next dc; rep from * across, ending last rep at ★★, dc in 3rd ch of tch, turn.

ROW 5: Ch 3 (counts as dc), 3 dc in first dc, *sk next 2 ch-3 sps, 4 dc in next dc, ch 3, sk next 3 dc, sc bet next 2 dc, ch 3, sk next 3 dc★★, 4 dc in next dc; rep from * across, ending last rep at ★★, dc in 3rd ch of tch, turn.

Rep rows 2-5 for patt.

Little Leaves

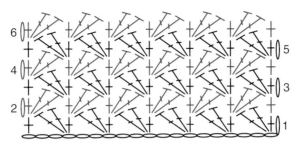

Chain a multiple of 3 plus 2.

ROW 1 (RS): (Sc, 2 dc) in 2nd ch from hook, ★sk next 2 ch, (sc, 2 dc) in next ch; rep from ★ across to within last 3 ch, sk next 2 ch, sc in last ch, turn.

ROW 2: Ch 1, (sc, 2 dc) in first sc, ★sk next 2 dc, (sc, 2 dc) in next sc; rep from ★ across to weithin last 3 sts, sk next 2 dc, sc in last sc, turn.

Rep row 2 for patt.

Angled Shells

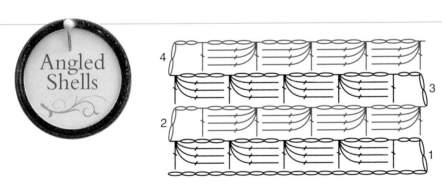

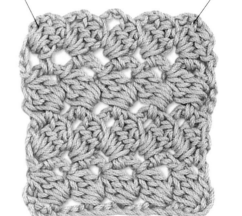

4-DC CLUSTER: Work 4 dc leaving last lp of each st on hook, yo, draw through all 5 lps.

Chain multiples of 4 plus 3.

ROW 1 (RS): Dc in 7th ch from hook, ★ch 3, work 4-dc cluster, working first 3 dc around the post of last dc made, sk next 3 ch, work 4th dc in next ch, complete cluster; rep from ★ across, turn.

ROW 2: Ch 5 (counts as dc, ch 2), dc in next ch-3 sp, ★ch 3, work 4-dc cluster, working first 3 dc around the post of last dc made, sk next cluster★★, work 4th dc in next ch-3 sp, complete cluster; rep from ★ across, ending last rep at ★★, sk next 2 ch of tch, work last dc of last cluster in next ch of tch, complete cluster, turn.

Rep row 2 for patt.

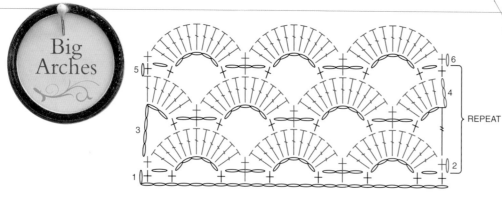

Big Arches

REPEAT

Chain a multiple of 8 plus 2 plus 1.

ROW 1 (WS): Sc in 2nd ch from hook, ch 1, sk next ch, sc in next ch, ★ch 5, sk next 3 ch, sc in next ch, ch 3, sk next 3 ch, sc in next ch; rep from ★ across to within last 7 ch, ch 5, sk next 3 ch, sc in next ch, ch 1, sk next ch, sc in last ch, turn.

ROW 2: Ch 1, sc in first sc, sk next ch–1 sp, ★11 dc in next ch–5 sp★★, working over next ch–3 sp, sc in center ch 2 rows below; rep from ★ across, ending last rep at ★★, sk next ch–1 sp, sc in last sc, turn.

ROW 3: Ch 6 (counts as tr, ch 2), sk first 4 sts, ★sc in next dc, ch 3, sk next 3 dc, sc in next dc★★, ch 5, sk next 7 sts; rep from ★ across, ending last rep at ★★, ch 2, sk next 3 dc, tr in last sc, turn.

ROW 4: Ch 3 (counts as dc), 5 dc in next ch–2 sp, ★working over next ch–3 sp, sc in center dc 2 rows below★★, 11 dc in next ch–5 sp; rep from ★ across, ending last rep at ★★, 5 dc in last ch–2 sp of tch, dc in 4th ch of tch, turn.

ROW 5: Ch 1, sc in first dc, ch 1, sk next dc, sc in next dc, ★ch 5, sk next 7 sts, sc in next dc★★, ch 3, sk next 3 dc, sc in next dc; rep from ★ across, ending last rep at ★★, ch 1, sk next dc, sc in top of tch.

Rep rows 2–5 for patt.

Buds in a Row

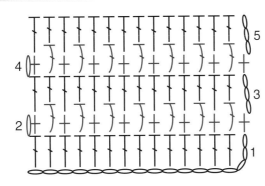

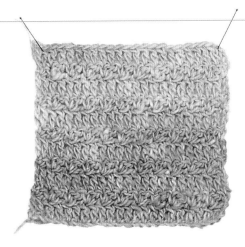

Chain multiples of 2 plus 1.

ROW 1 (RS): Dc in 4th ch from hook and in ea ch across, turn.

ROW 2: Ch 1, sc in first dc, ★dc in next sc, sc in next dc; rep from ★ across, ending with last sc in top of tch, turn.

ROW 3: Ch 3 (counts as dc), sk first dc, dc in ea st across, turn.

Rep rows 2–3 for patt.

Wavy Shell

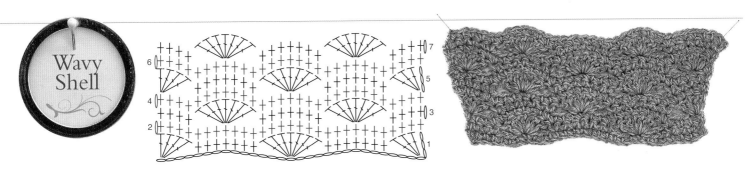

Chain multiples of 14 plus 4.

ROW 1 (RS): 3 dc in 4th ch from hook, ★sk next 3 ch, sc in ea of next 7 ch, sk next 3 ch★★, 7 dc in next ch; rep from ★ across, ending last rep at ★★, 4 dc in last ch, turn.

ROW 2: Ch 1, sc in ea st across, sc in top of tch, turn.

ROW 3: Ch 1, sc in each of first 4 sc, ★sk next 3 sc, 7 dc in next sc, sk next 3 sc, sc in ea of next 7 sc; rep from ★ across, ending with sc in ea of last 4 sc, turn.

ROW 4: Rep row 2.

ROW 5: Ch 3 (counts as dc), 3 dc in first sc, ★sk next 3 sc, sc in ea of next 7 sc, sk next 3 sc★★, 7 dc in next ch; rep from ★ across, ending last rep at ★★, 4 dc in last sc, turn.

Rep rows 2–5 for patt.

Open Crossed Cables

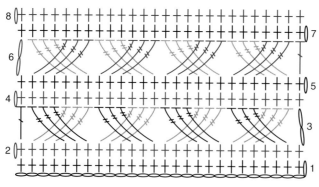

Chain multiples of 6 plus 3.

ROW 1 (RS): Sc in 2nd ch from hook and in ea ch across, turn.

ROW 2: Ch 1, sc in ea sc across, turn.

ROW 3: Ch 2 (counts as dc), sk first sc, *sk next 3 sc, tr in ea of next 3 sc, working over last 3 tr made, tr in first skipped sc, tr in ea of next 2 skipped sc; rep from * across to within last sc, dc in last sc, turn.

ROW 4: Ch 1, sc in ea st across, ending with sc in top of tch, turn.

Rep rows 2-4 for patt.

Puffs and V's

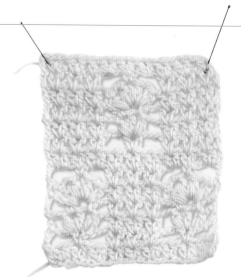

DC3TOG: Work dc in next st or sp, leaving last lp of ea st on hook, yo, draw through all 4 lps.

V-ST: (Dc, ch 1, dc) in same st or sp.

Chain a multiple of 18 plus 1.

ROW 1 (RS): V-st in 5th ch from hook, *sk next 2 ch, V-st in next ch; rep from * across to within last 2 ch, sk next ch, dc in last ch, turn.

ROW 2: Ch 3 (counts as dc), sk first 2 dc, V-st in next V-st, *ch 3, sk next V-st, V-st in next V-st, ch 3, sk next V-st**, V-st in ea of next 3 V-sts; rep from * across, ending last rep at **, V-st in last V-st, dc in top of tch, turn.

ROW 3: Ch 3 (counts as dc), sk first 2 dc, V-st in next V-st, *ch 1, sk next ch-3 sp, (dc3tog, ch 2, dc, ch 2, dc3tog) in next V-st, ch 1, sk next ch-3 sp**, V-st in ea of next 3 V-sts; rep from * across, ending last rep at **, V-st in last V-st, dc in top of tch, turn.

Puffs and V's

continued

ROW 4: Ch 3 (counts as dc), sk first 2 dc, V-st in next V-st, ★ch 3, sk next ch-1 sp, (sc, ch 3) in ea of next 2 ch-2 sps, sk next ch-1 sp★★, V-st in ea of next 3 V-sts; rep from ★ across, ending last rep at ★★, V-st in last V-st, dc in top of tch, turn.

ROW 5: Ch 3 (counts as dc), sk first 2 dc, V-st in next V-st, ★ch 2, sk next ch-3 sp, (dc3tog, ch 3) 3 times in next ch-3 sp, dc3tog in same ch-3 sp, ch 2, sk next ch-3 sp★★, V-st in ea of next 3 V-sts; rep from ★ across, ending last rep at ★★, V-st in last V-st, dc in top of tch, turn.

ROW 6: Ch 3 (counts as dc), sk first 2 dc, V-st in next V-st, ★ch 4, sk next 2 ch-sps, sc in next ch-3 sp, ch 4, sk next 2 ch-sps★★, V-st in ea of next 3 V-sts; rep from ★ across, ending last rep at ★★, V-st in last V-st, dc in top of tch, turn.

ROW 7: Ch 3 (counts as dc), sk first 2 dc, V-st in next V-st, ★V-st in next ch-4 sp, V-st in next sc, V-st in next ch-4 sp★★, V-st in ea of next 3 V-sts; rep from ★ across, ending last rep at ★★, V-st in last V-st, dc in top of tch, turn.

ROW 8: Ch 3 (counts as dc), sk first 2 dc, V-st in ea of next 4 V-sts, ★ch 3, sk next V-st, V-st in next V-st, ch 3, sk next V-st, V-st in ea of next 3 V-sts; rep from ★ across to within last V-st, V-st in last V-st, dc in top of tch, turn.

ROW 9: Ch 3 (counts as dc), sk first 2 dc, V-st in ea of next 4 V-sts, ★ch 1, sk next ch-3 sp, (dc3tog, ch 2, dc, ch 2, dc3tog) in next V-st, ch 1, sk next ch-3 sp, V-st in ea of next 3 V-sts; rep from ★ across to within last V-st, V-st in last V-st, dc in top of tch, turn.

ROW 10: Ch 3 (counts as dc), sk first 2 dc, V-st in ea of next 4 V-sts, ★ch 3, sk next ch-1 sp, (sc, ch 3) in ea of next 2 ch-2 sps, sk next ch-1 sp, V-st in ea of next 3 V-sts; rep from ★ across to within last V-st, V-st in last V-st, dc in top of tch, turn.

ROW 11: Ch 3 (counts as dc), sk first 2 dc, V-st in ea of next 4 V-sts, ★ch 2, sk next ch-3 sp, (dc3tog, ch 3) 3 times in next ch-3 sp, dc3tog in same ch-3 sp, ch 2, sk next ch-3 sp, V-st in ea of next 3 V-sts; rep from ★ across to within last V-st, V-st in last V-st, dc in top of tch, turn.

ROW 12: Ch 3 (counts as dc), sk first 2 dc, V-st in ea of next 4 V-sts, ★ch 4, sk next 2 ch-sps, sc in next ch-3 sp, ch 4, sk next 2 ch-sps, V-st in ea of next 3 V-sts; rep from ★ across to within last V-st, V-st in last V-st, dc in top of tch, turn.

ROW 13: Ch 3 (counts as dc), sk first 2 dc, V-st in ea of next 4 V-sts, ★V-st in next ch-4 sp, V-st in next sc, V-st in next ch-4 sp, V-st in ea of next 3 V-sts; rep from ★ across to within last V-st, V-st in last V-st, dc in top of tch, turn

Rep rows 2-13 for patt.

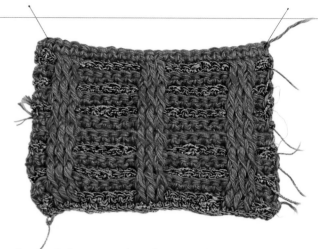

FPDC: Yo, insert hook from front around post of corresponding st 2 rows below, complete dc as usual. Note: FPdc's in row 3 will be worked around the posts of corresponding sc's in row 1. FPdc's in later rows will be worked around the posts of corresponding FPdc's 2 rows below.

Worked in 2 colors, A and B

With A, ch a multiple of 10 plus 7 plus 1

ROW 1 (RS): Sc in 2nd ch from hook and in ea ch across, turn, change to B.

ROW 2: Ch 1, FLsc in ea sc across, turn, change to A.

ROW 3: Ch 1, FLsc in first 2 sc, *FPdc in ea of next 3 sts 2 rows below, FLsc in ea of next 7 sc; rep from * across to within last 5 sts, ending with FPdc in ea of next 3 sts 2 rows below, FLsc in ea of last 2 sts, turn, change to B.

ROWS 4-7: Rep rows 2 and 3 twice. Do not change to B at end of last row.

ROWS 8-9: With A, rep rows 2 and 3. At end of Row 9, change to B.

ROW 10: Rep row 2.

Rep rows 3–10 for patt.

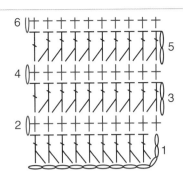

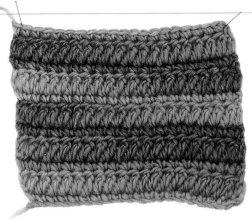

Forked Cluster Stitch

Forked cluster (FC): (Yo, insert hook in next ch or st as indicated, yo, draw yarn through st) twice, (yo, draw yarn through 3 lps on hook) twice.

Ch any number

ROW 1 (RS): Starting in 3rd ch from hook, FC in next 2 ch, ★FC worked in same ch as last FC and next ch; rep from across, turn.

ROW 2: Ch 1, sc in ea st across, sc in top of tch.

ROW 3: Ch 2, FC in first and 2nd sc, ★FC worked in same sc at last FC and in next sc; rep from ★ across, turn.

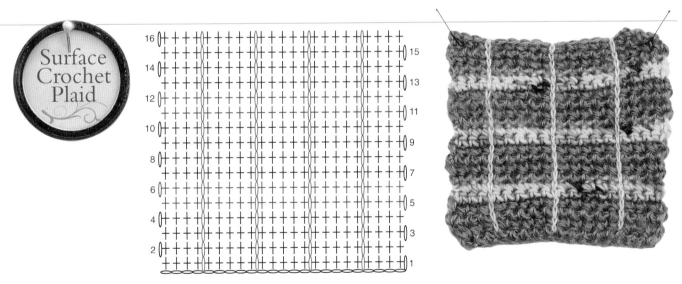

Surface Crochet Plaid

Worked in 3 Colors, A, B and C (a finer weight of yarn).

With A, chain a multiple of 5 plus 3 plus 1.

ROW 1 (RS): Sc in 2nd ch from hook and in ea ch across, turn.

ROW 2: Ch 1, sc in ea sc across, turn.

Rep row 2 working in the following color sequence: 2 more rows A, ★2 rows B, 4 rows A; rep from ★ for desired length.

SURFACE CROCHET: With C, work a row of surface crochet chains vertically, one chain per row, between the 4th and 5th st from edge of piece, ★sk next 5 sc, work next vertical row of surface crochet between next 2 sts; rep from ★ across width of piece. There should be 4 sc left at opposite side after final vertical row.

Herring-bone look

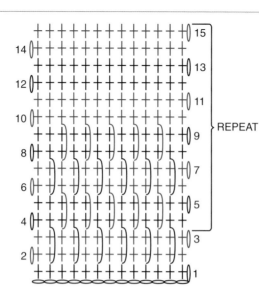

REPEAT

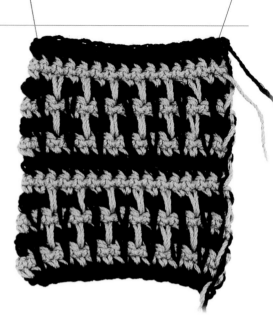

Note: Rows will appear slightly offset to right (or left for left-handers) but if you stick to your stitch count the patt will work out as shown.

SSC3: Work over 2 rows, sc in top of st 3 rows below – which will be the same color as working row.

2 colors, A and B, colors carried along side

With A, chain an even number sts (loosely)

ROW 1 (RS): Sc in 2nd ch from hook and in ea ch across, turn. Change to B.

ROWS 2-3: Ch 1, sc in ea sc across, turn. Change to A.

ROW 4: Ch 1, sc in first sc, ★Ssc3 in next sc 3 rows below, sc in next sc; rep from ★ across, turn.

ROW 5: Ch 1, sc in ea st across, turn, change to B,

ROW 6: Ch 1, sc in first 2 sc, ★Ssc3 in next sc 3 rows below, sc in next sc; rep from ★ across to within last st, sc in last sc, turn. Change to A,.

ROW 7: Ch 1, sc in ea st across, turn.

ROW 8-11: Rep rows 4-7. Change to B.

ROWS 12-13: Ch 1, sc in ea st across, turn. Change to A.

ROWS 14-15: Ch 1, sc in ea st across, turn.

Rep rows 4-15 for patt.

Loop Stitch

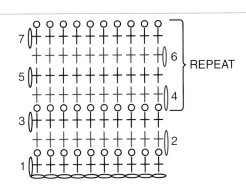

REPEAT

Chain any number

ROW 1 (WS): Loop st in 2nd ch from hook and in ea ch across, turn.

ROW 2: Ch 1, sc in ea st across, turn.

ROW 3: Ch 1, loop st in ea sc across, turn.

ROWS 4-6: Rep row 2.

ROW 7: Rep row 3.

Rep rows 4-7 for patt.

A basic loop stitch is made by wrapping the yarn around a finger, then securing it with a single crochet. Unlike fur stitches, the loop in this case is a single strand of yarn.

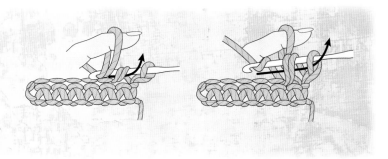

Chain Fur Stitch

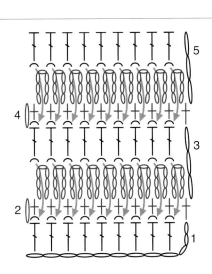

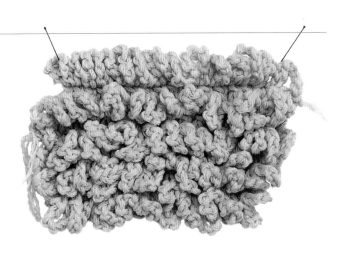

Chain any number

ROW 1 (RS): Dc in 4th ch and in ea ch across.

ROW 2: Ch 1, BLsc in first dc, ★ch 7, BLsc in next dc, rep from ★ across, ending with sc in top of tch.

ROW 3: Ch 3 (counts as dc), working behind sts in row 2, dc in rem back lp of next st of row 1. Rep rows 2 and 3 for patt.

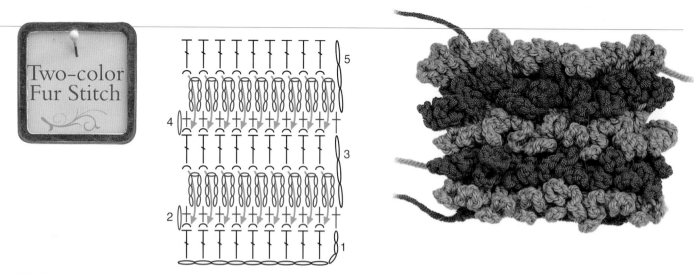

Two-color Fur Stitch

Work same as Chain Fur Stitch but change color at the end of every odd-numbered row. Work in the following color sequence: ★2 rows A, 2 rows B; rep from ★ throughout.

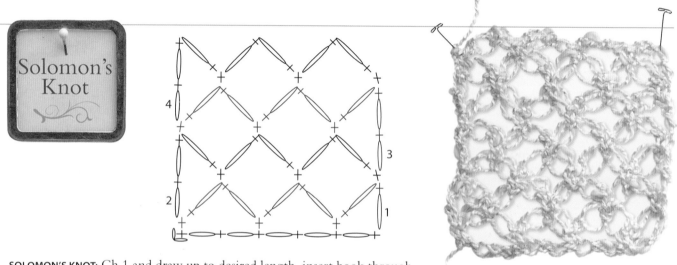

Solomon's Knot

SOLOMON'S KNOT: Ch 1 and draw up to desired length, insert hook through back loop of ch just made, yo, draw through lp, yo, draw yarn through 2 loops on hook (sc made).

MAIN SOLOMON'S KNOT (MSK): Solomon's knots used for the body of the fabric. They are 1½ times as long as ESK sts. For this example, make the ch approx ¾" long.

EDGE SOLOMON'S KNOT (ESK): Solomon's knots used for the foundation "chain" and the "turning chains" or edge sts. They are ⅔ the length of MSK sts. For this example make the ch approx ½" long.

FOUNDATION CHAIN: Ch 2, sc in 2nd ch from hook, work a multiple of 2 ESK, turn.

ROW 1 (RS): Work 2 MSK, sc between 3rd and 4th sc from hook, ★work 2 MSK, sk 2 loops, sc in next sc; rep from ★ across to last sc, turn.

ROW 2: Work 2 ESK and 1 MSK, sc between 4th and 5th sc from hook, ★work 2 MSK, sk 2 loops, sc in next sc; rep from ★ across, turn.

Rep row 2 for patt.

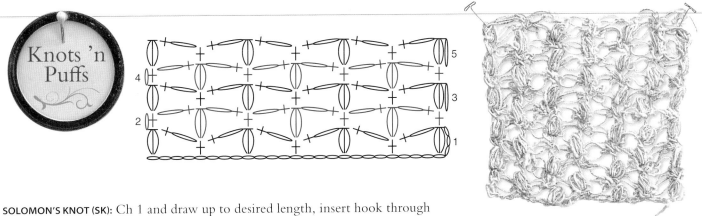

Knots 'n Puffs

SOLOMON'S KNOT (SK): Ch 1 and draw up to desired length, insert hook through back lp of ch just made, yo, draw through lp, yo, draw yarn through 2 lps on hook (sc made).

PUFF ST: (Yo, draw up a lp) 3 times in same st, yo and draw through all 7 lps on hook, ch 1 tightly to closed.

Chain a multiple of 8 plus 4

ROW 1: Puff st in 4th ch from hook, ★SK, sk next 3 ch, sc in next ch, SK, sk 3 ch, puff st in next ch; rep from ★ across, turn.

ROW 2: Ch 1, sc in first puff st, ★SK, sk next lp, puff st in next sc, SK, sk next lp, sc in next puff st; rep from ★ across, turn.

ROW 3: Ch 1, puff st in first sc, ★SK, sk next lp, sc in puff st, SK, sk next lp, puff in next sc; rep from ★ across, turn.

Rep rows 2-3 for patt.

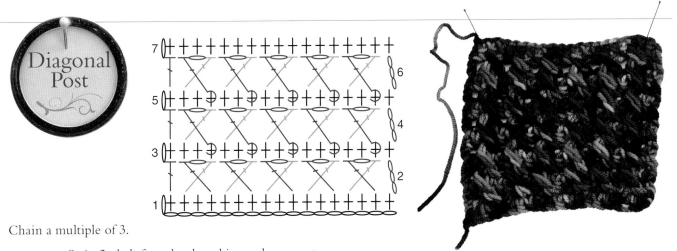

Diagonal Post

Chain a multiple of 3.

ROW 1 (WS): Sc in 2nd ch from hook and in ea ch across, turn.

ROW 2: Ch 3 (counts as dc), sk first sc, ★sk next 2 sc, dc in next sc, ch 1, working over last dc made, dc in first of 2 skipped sc; rep from ★ across to within last sc, dc in last sc, turn.

ROW 3: Ch 1, sc in each dc and ch-1 sp across, turn.

Rep rows 2-3 for patt.

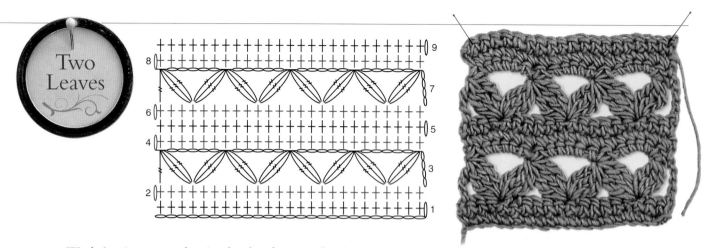

TR3TOG: Work 3 tr in same st, leaving last lp of ea st on hook, yo, draw through all 4 lps.

6-TR CLUSTER: Work 3 tr in next st, leaving last lp of ea st on hook, sk next 5 sc, work 3 tr in next st, leaving last lp of ea st on hook, yo, draw through all 7 lps.

4-TR CLUSTER: Work 3 tr in next st, leaving last lp of ea st on hook, sk next 2 sc, work tr in next st, leaving last lp of ea st on hook, yo, draw through all 5 lps.

Chain multiples of 6 plus 2.

ROW 1 (RS): Sc in 2nd ch from hook and in ea ch across, turn.

ROW 2: Ch 1, sc in ea sc across, turn.

ROW 3: Ch 4 (counts as tr), sk first 3 sc, tr3tog in next sc, ★ch 5, work 6-tr cluster, working first 3 tr, in same sc as last cluster, sk next 5 sc, work next 3 tr in next sc, complete cluster; rep from ★ across to within last 3 sts, ch 5, work 4-tr cluster, working first 3 tr in same st as last cluster, sk next 2 sc, work last tr in last sc, complete cluster, turn.

ROW 4: Ch 1, sc in first cluster, ★5 sc in next ch-5 sp, sc in next cluster; rep from ★ across, turn.

ROW 5: Ch 1, sc in ea sc across, turn.

Rep rows 2-5 for patt.

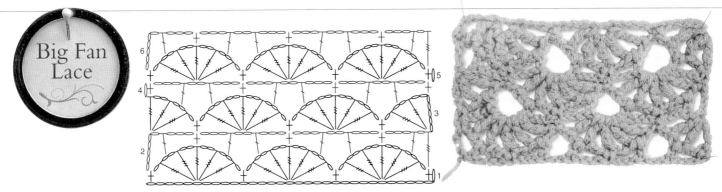

FAN: (Dtr, ch 2) 4 times in next st or sp, dtr in same st or sp.

Chain multiples of 10 plus 2.

ROW 1 (RS): Sc in 2nd ch from hook, *ch 1, sk next 4 ch, Fan in next ch, ch 1, sk next 4 ch, sc in next ch; rep from * across, turn.

ROW 2: Ch 6 (counts as dtr, ch 1), sk next ch-1 sp, *dc in next ch-2 sp, ch 3, sk next ch-2 sp, sc in next dtr, ch 3, sk next ch-2 sp, dc in next ch-2 sp**, ch 2, sk next 2 ch-1 sps; rep from * across, ending last rep at **, ch 1, dtr in last sc, turn.

ROW 3: Ch 7 (counts as dtr, ch 2), (dtr, ch 2, dtr) in first dtr, ch 1, sk next ch-1 sp, *sk next ch-3 sp, sc in next sc, ch 1, sk next ch-3 sp**, Fan in next ch-2 sp; rep from * across, ending last rep at **, (dtr, ch 2, dtr, ch 2, dtr) in 5th ch of tch, turn.

ROW 4: Ch 1, sc in first dtr, *ch 3, sk next ch-2 sp, dc in next ch-2 sp, ch 2, sk next 2 ch-1 sps, dc in next ch-2 sp, ch 3, skip next ch-2 sp**, sc in next dtr; rep from * across, ending last rep at ** sc in 5th ch of tch, turn.

ROW 5: Ch 1, sc in first sc, *ch 1, sk next ch-3 sp, Fan in next ch-2 sp, ch 1, sk next ch-3 sp, sc in next sc; rep from * across, turn.

Rep rows 2-5 for patt.

US VS UK CROCHET TERMS

US	UK
chain(ch)	chain(ch)
single crochet (sc)	double crochet (dc)
double crochet (dc)	treble (tr)
half double crochet (hdc)	half treble (htr)
triple crochet (trc)	double treble (dtr)
slip stitch (sl st)	slip stitch (sl st)

CROCHET ABBREVIATION CHART

This table lists some common crochet abbreviations. Each pattern also includes a list of stitches and techniques used, with their abbreviations.

ABBREVIATION	DESCRIPTION
()	repeat the instructions in the parentheses the number of times specified
*	repeat the instructions after the * as instructed
approx	approximately
beg	begin(ning)
BLO	back loop(s) only
ch(s)	chain(s)
cm	centimeter(s)
dc	double crochet(s)
dec	decrease(-ing)
FLO	front loop(s) only
FPdc	front post double crochet
g	gram(s)
hdc	half double crochet(s)
inc	increase
invdec	invisible decrease
lp(s)	loop(s)
m	meter(s)
mr	make ring
oz	ounce(s)
patt	pattern
RS	right side(s)
rem	remain(ing)
rep	repeat(ing)
rnd(s)	round(s)
sc	single crochet(s)
sc2tog	single crochet 2 together
sk	skip
sl st	slip stitch(es)
st(s)	stitch(es)
tog	together
tr	treble crochet(s), (sometimes called triple crochet)
WS	wrong side(s)
yd	yard(s)
YO	yarn over hook

STITCH KEY

- ⬭ = chain (ch)
- • = slip stitch (sl st)
- ✚ = single crochet (sc)
- ⊤ = half double crochet (hdc)
- ⊤ = double crochet (dc)
- ⊤ = treble crochet (tr)
- ⊤ = double treble crochet (dtr)
- ⬭✚ = Solomon's knot (SK, MSK or ESK)
- ⬭⬭ = surface crochet
- ⊥ = loop st
- ⊥ = FPsc or SFPsc
- ✚✚✚✚ = Spike sts (Ssc2, Ssc3, Ssc4, Ssc5)
- ⬭ = puff st
- ⬭ = 3-dc puff
- ⬭ = sideways bobble (dc5tog)

 = Ch 4-CL (ch 4, tr2tog)

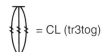 = CL (tr3tog)

 = 4-tr cluster

 = 6-tr cluster

 = dtr2tog

 = dtr3tog

⋏ = sc2tog

⅂ = forked cluster (FC)

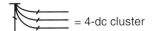 = 4-dc cluster

⊤ = 2-tr cluster

⋏ = tr2tog

 = tr3tog

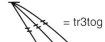 = tr7tog

 = tr4tog

⊤ = front post dc (FPdc)

⊤ = back post dc (BPdc)

 = roundel

⊤ = Extended dc (Exdc)

✕ = crossed dc

 = V-st

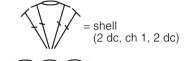 = shell (2 dc, ch 1, 2 dc)

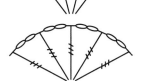

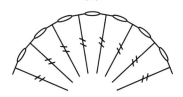

⬭ = ch-3 picot

⌒ = worked in back loop only

⌣ = worked in front loop only

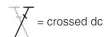

Acknowledgments

My list of people to thank is short and very sweet: Leslie Johnson for her help with sewing instructions. Nancy Smith, Yvonne Cherry, and Mary Dubois for their great stitching. I am also very grateful for the generosity of several yarn companies who donated yarns for swatches and projects: Aslan Trends, Beroco, Caron, Coats & Clark, Colinette, Lion Brand, Louet, Punta Yarns, Skacel, Urban GypZ, Tahki Stacey Charles, Trendsetter, and Universal Yarns. I'd like to give special thanks to my editor, Terry Taylor, for his wisdom and encouragement all along the way.

About the Author

Dora Ohrenstein pursued a career as a classically trained singer for 30 years, touring internationally and making many recordings before she returned to her crochet. She began designing crochet fashions, first for herself, and subsequently for publication. Her designs have been shown in the magazines *Interweave Crochet*, *knit.1*, and *Crochet Today!*; the books *The New Crochet*, and *Fabulous Crocheted Ponchos* (both from Lark Books); and in several books by Rita Weiss. She is the author of the book *Crochet Insider's Passion for Fashion*, published in 2008 by Leisure Arts. Dora is founder and editor of the webzine *Crochet Insider* (www.crochtinsider.com), which features interviews of industry leaders and textile artists, book and yarn reviews, and galleries of creative crochet from designers from across the globe. She lives and works in Manhattan, where in addition to designing, she teaches singing.

Index